Variance: An Inductive  n
in Social I

Christopher Donnelly, PhD

About the Author

Christopher Donnelly received his PhD in Sociology from the University of Connecticut in 2015. He currently lives in Vermont, USA.

Contents

I) An Introduction

In *The Myth of Sisyphus*, Albert Camus outlines a philosophy that transcends nihilism and existentialism. In its pages, he develops the concept of the *absurd* and examines the methods used to cope with this condition. I use these notions as a starting point for this analysis. This book ignores Camus' later work[1], and expands his method of thought beyond the sociological and practical implications in *The Myth*. Specifically, this work applies Camus' method to the human mind by examining its cognitive processes and their consequences. This work not only expands the applicability of Absurdism. It also increases understanding of man's interpretation of the natural world and his place in it.

This book is written to be as widely accessible as possible and requires little prior knowledge of Absurdism. That said, I strongly suggest reading (and understanding) *The Myth of Sisyphus* prior to this work. This book also moves fast (especially initially), and refrains from dwelling on any topic for an extensive period of time. It includes some scientific concepts that may prove confusing to a general audience. I apologize in advance, and provide extensive footnotes to elucidate any concepts that may be troublesome. These also direct the reader to additional resources.

Each of the chapters in this text should be understood as building upon one another, yet they also have their individual merits. As I discuss in extensive detail, a hallmark of the natural and social worlds is their contradictory character, and those of you who seek inconsistency in this analysis will find it. This is not a concern of either the method or content in this book.

Lastly, I encourage the reader to remember this is a scientific text. While composed in a more 'mainstream'

---

[1] *The Rebel* is an application of Camus' methodology in *The Myth* to human behavior. This book examines a different topic.

polemical style, it is an inductive study of human experience with specific objectives. Social themes are occasionally objects of analysis. There is no value judgement implied during these analyses — the absurdist method is uninterested in such things. If offense occurs, it was not intended. Certain past experiences urge me to make this clear.

-C. Donnelly

II) Premise

The absurd condition is often treated as an external phenomenon. It is man's confrontation with a world beyond his understanding that constrains his action. This natural world stands outside of him and opposes him. He either eludes his awareness of this situation or attempts to defy this world. While *The Myth of Sisyphus* includes some discussion on how this opaque natural world restricts man's understanding of himself, this topic remains significantly underdeveloped. In this text, I analyze the absurd condition beyond action and lifestyle. I seek to understand how the absurd impacts our cognition and our interpretation of reality. I do this by focusing on the structure and process of the human mind.

This study utilizes the same methodology as *The Myth*. It strives to analyze "without appeal" through an inductive framework[2]. The basis of this method is the refusal of assumptions and reliance on naked evidence. It is thoroughly anti-theoretical and attempts to avoid giving the world *depth* by relying on this or that 'system' for organizing and comprehending it. All systems and theories are based on assumptions, and I strive to make as few as possible.

A technique for rejecting assumptions is the deliberate avoidance of other works. Inductive methodology requires keeping an open mind above all else and examining other studies can jeopardize this orientation. While this method is somewhat drastic and beyond what I normally recommend, I feel it necessary when examining a topic researched so prolifically. Accordingly, this study will not use or make note of any other Absurdist text other than its foundational work,

---

[2] See page 53 in *The Myth* for Camus' idea of living without appeal. Inductive research generates new ideas about a social process, while deductive methodologies apply pre-existing theory to a process.

The Myth of Sisyphus. Other works outside this tradition are discussed only for comparison.

Methodology aside, this analysis requires some conceptual starting point. While largely a method, Absurdism does have some key conclusions. Camus outlines two — a) I exist, and b) the world outside me exists, but the *quality* of both is largely unknown to me. While I can explain the natural world to some extent (for instance, gravity on Earth), when I look beyond the immediate present everything becomes unclear; unreasonable; contradictory. Camus provides examples of this in *The Myth* (as do armies of intellectuals and doctoral students), so a rather elementary example may be permitted here.

Right now, I am looking at a mug on my desk. I touch it. It is ceramic, hard, and unyielding. It does not appear to move at all, nor vary from its cylindrical shape. But these assertions are a matter of *perception*. Basic physics tells me this mug is just an arrangement of molecules which themselves are an arrangement of atoms[3]. These atoms, supposedly, are constantly moving to this-or-that degree depending on this-or-that confounding effect (for instance, temperature). But I do not see this movement, nor do I understand it in my immediate perception.

This does not mean my perception is flawed, or science is completely correct. Atomic theory is based on some rather significant assumptions regarding matter and energy. These assumptions are challenged by Nature and other concepts such as black holes and dark matter. What is important in this situation is the multiple explanations regarding the 'nature' of this mug — my perception and a theoretical perception. Both invariably change; my eyesight will decline and cause the mug to appear fuzzy and even more uniform, and science is always striving to adjust its theories and expand its knowledge. What matters in this example is the confusion

---

[3] For an excellent introduction to elementary physics, see Feynman et al. (1977).

and *multiplicity* of perspectives. Neither explanation is 'right' per se, for both are constantly changing. They are approximations, and as such will never reveal the 'true' nature of this mug.

This drive to understand the relatively non-understandable is a central manifestation of the absurd condition in humanity. This condition demands an explanation.

The absurd is a *relationship* between humanity and the world. On one side is Man and his desire to understand. He wishes to unify the world and make it completely perceptible. He wants it to wholly and consistently abide by his ideas. He posits moral mandates about how it should behave and exist.

On the other side of this relationship is the natural world. Nature is above all *unreasonable*, opaque, and significantly *contradictory*. It is a world that commonly resists us, that does not allow us to fully understand its behavior or content. Note the word "fully" in the previous sentence. While our theorems may explain the world to some extent, they are severely limited in their applicability. They can explain phenomenon in one instance under a certain set of conditions with a certain set of assumptions, yet when these conditions and assumptions are broken the world acts in a contradictory fashion. This is what Camus means by the notion of *limit* as a check to scientific explanation[4].

For example, there is that universal blackguard known as *time* which limits the applicability of these cute little theories dreamt up in dusty academic offices. Time can impact systems of thought. For instance, a decade of time often leads to significant changes in social science theory. Time is also incorporated into theory as an attempt to control it. Take physical science. Astrophysics assumes an expanding universe (on what and into what no one really knows), and this expansion only takes place because time progresses. This

---

[4] See page 36 in *The Myth*.

theory rests on the assertion that all matter comes from somewhere after something (the 'big bang' for instance), and the implicit assumption is other events could alter this process (the universe could 'hit a wall' and simply stop expanding). I do not know if this will happen...do you? By attempting to control Nature theoretically, more questions arise than are answered. Science becomes an exercise in art and creation rather than empiricism and observation.

Whenever you look long enough at even the most basic assumptions in contemporary science and society, assumptions fall apart. Everything, in short, leads to confusion.

Faced with this situation, a vast majority of mankind run from it. Why wouldn't they? As I discuss later, the human mind thrives on basic assumptions, desires, and moral platitudes. When confronted with the vast complexity of human and natural existence, almost all minds instantaneously recoil from this awareness and plunge their thoughts into this-or-that. These are what Camus calls "elusions". They are provided by Society and necessary for its survival.

The natural aspect of your mind also provides these ideas to support your existence. Concerned with your survival, it supports an extraordinary myopia that inflates your sense of masterfulness and perceived capacity to shape the world. Think of elusions as, say, alcohol. Alcohol numbs you to stimuli from the outside world; it drives your consciousness internally. Limiting your perception, it makes you more agreeable to social conversation with others (and thereby more likely to support their elusions), strengthens your sense of personal veracity, and limits your immediate experience of the consequences of your thoughts and actions. In addition, it washes over you with a pleasant drowsiness; what a beautiful little distraction. Excess leads to illness, but for many this illness is preferable to reality. It is an acceptable risk.

This is how elusions operate. Cultural norms, religion, subcultures, even language limit and manipulate your perception. If current theory is believed, it is relatively impossible for us with our barely evolved apeish minds to ever experience reality in its naked clarity[5]. Our language limits us, our beliefs limit us, our culture limits us, and our connections to others limit us (just to mention a few). Everything leads to confusion. Elusion is the embrace of confusion — not the kind of confusion that confuses in the common sense of the word, but the kind of confusion that confuses the natural world and ourselves into something far more pleasant, easy, comforting, and desirable.

I do not blame the vast majority of humanity who sniff the roses and eat the poppies of elusion. Neither should you. You probably live this way now. I often wish I could live this way now. I tried multiple times over the years, but the unshakable tension of the absurd drew me back. Such is life.

This alludes to another theme in this text. The analyses and ideas presented here are *dangerous*. I do not intend to sound overly dramatic, nor to infuse this text with a sense of *sexiness* to enhance your intake of its ideas. What I intend is to sufficiently touch upon the consequences of Camus' thought. The path of the Absurdist (if there is such a person), or more correctly of the *True Scientist*, requires stripping away all the fancy ideas and notions you once held dear; not only about how the world works, but about yourself as well. The absurd method requires grabbing yourself by the scruff and ripping your head from the swamp of elusion. It requires letting go of all belief, especially about how you think the world works and your place in it. You must also let go of beliefs about yourself — beliefs in your intelligence and ability; in any kind of *process* leading you through life, religious or otherwise. What is required is perceiving as much as you can as clearly

---

[5] For an excellent analysis of meaning embedded in concepts necessary for comprehending reality, See Foucault's *Discipline and Punish* (1995).

as you can. The limits to this orientation are known[6]. They descend from our lackluster development in comparison to animals. But the Absurdist has an unreconcilable taste for truth. *Clean* truth, not only that which supports a scientist or philosopher's pet system.

Allow me to apologize for pedantry. Revealing the assumptions and limits of science is a favorite pastime of philosophers and social constructionists throughout academia. They have luncheons about it. Usually physical science is the primary target. Any angst thrown at them versus social science is merely on account of 'basic' science's vanity. Physical science is populated with individuals so confident in the importance and necessity of their various expeditions into the natural. When the absurd condition is maintained however, the *True Scientist* sees that "everything is permitted"[7]. The only criterion that makes physical science more important than social in western society is the belief that it is, indeed, more important. It is easier to look without than within, and Society often prefers explaining the movement of dirt or the melding of steel than the inequalities radiating throughout its system[8].

I've done it again! Another foray into pedantry. Allow me to tie this up quickly. My hostility with science is simple; it usually does not behave like science. Absurdism seeks to examine and explain the world only with those truths that are self-evident and without assumption. Science — both social and physical — embraces assumption and propagates it. The sure way for a budding academic to make his mark is to invent some new system based off a slew of other systems.

---

[6] As Camus says consciousness must be "caught on the wing, at that barely perceptible moment when it glances fleetingly at itself" (1991: 77).

[7] See *The Myth*, page 67.

[8] I do not intend to portray society as a living being. By all measure there is no central consciousness to society. It is not an autonomous life form as far as I can tell. It does, however, tend to perpetuate itself though the actions of individuals in its institutions. See Max Weber's (1958) work on bureaucracy for further explanation.

This reduces the likelihood of offending this person or that. Science, especially *social* science, is now intellectual diplomacy. Academics seek to appease and inflate their egos by supporting each other's theories via merging and building on them. This is the key, any prospective scholars out there, to getting your PhD.

Diatribes aside, let me caution that the processes described in this chapter are already explained in Camus' work. My all-to-brief summary of their characteristics exists merely to introduce them to the reader. Additionally, this work is a snapshot of my current thinking, a single point during my continuing study of human existence. It will change, and perhaps even be contradicted in the future. Such is the nature, you will see, of existence.

Now then, on to other things. No idea should go unpunished, even the author's favorite one. Critiques are as necessary to the inquiring mind as water is to the sea. Let us see if I can swamp the boat.

III) Critiques of this Premise

Perhaps my favorite critique of Absurdism is *it doesn't matter*. It is a worthless philosophy that has no footing in the 'real' world. Such arguments are often utilitarian in origin, and especially favored by those in physical sciences and/or the eluded. The crux of this argument is the supposed lack of impact absurdist ideas have on the operation of society and the natural world. In capitalist societies, the measure of an idea can often (but not always) be measured in its applicability for profit. In this light, absurdist ideas are indeed worthless, aside from their utility for selling books to students and self-proclaimed intellectuals. Nothing *The Myth* posits turns a profit, and, in fact, it is probably more likely to cause an individual to turn away from profitable diversions in society.

Some who traverse the absurdist realm may take issue with this argument. For instance, in Camus' *A Happy Death*, the main character Mersault achieved a prototypical 'beautiful' life according to the author. Happily spending the money of the man he murdered, Mersault devotes the rest of his years to living a blissful life without elusion or want. In this case, even though the spirit of the text is far from capitalist, the absurdist still nudges along the gears of production and fulfills his economic mandate. Sure, Mersault sought happiness through solitude at the book's end, but this was only possible because of the wealth he acquired and spent. But this interpretation is a rather sick inversion of thought from the man who wrote *The Rebel*, and is rather amusingly superficial and naive. The absurdist method, in its pure form, does not care about capitalism any more than anything else — placing this economic system on a moral alter as the best form of social organization is a value judgement foreign to its orbit.

This utilitarian critique does not, however, damage the use of Absurdism for understanding the natural and social worlds. With the later, Society can be viewed as both based on elusions and requiring them for its existence. Societies and their institutions provide no poverty of meanings to guide one's life, and any society can be 'worth dying for'. When considering the natural world Absurdism shows, as asserted by Camus, that if science is not to devolve into art and artifice, if it is to shun theory and stick solely with what it knows, then it is reduced to the level of description. Creating a taxonomy of this natural process or that natural process is not such a waste of time as the physicist or biologist will have you believe. In my opinion, it is of greater 'utility' to catalogue natural phenomenon than to supposedly explain it by theories based on assumptions and drawings.

Another critique: this time from the moralists and those who fancy themselves immoralists (but are really still moralists). Beginning with the later, Camus addresses many of these individuals during his critique of Existentialism and Phenomenology. These 'free thinkers' as they often credit themselves can indeed perform an exquisite job outlining the apparent meaninglessness and baseness of all existence. However, as Camus shows, shortly after their long, convoluted proofs demonstrating man's tormented state of being, they 'leap' away from it and rush into this-or-that system of meaning[9]. Judases of the intellect, their assertions that the world is meaningless only increase their desire to escape it.

Now *moralists* on the other hand are especially prominent in contemporary society, thanks to Post Modernism, Third Wave Feminism, and Post Structuralist currents in academia. Marxism, once the herald of unavoidable change and the vanguard of counterculture is

---

[9] 'System of Meaning' is a common term in social constructionist traditions. For the purposes of this book, I define it as a lens or perspective individuals use to interpret the world.

attacked by these traditions for supporting social categories that suppress groups in society, such as women[10]. Now the countercultural fad is to deconstruct systems of meaning that reinforce systems of oppression. This is most exemplified at the time of this writing with the transsexual movement and their deconstruction of traditional gender and sexual categories. While these movements may indeed be disrupting systems of meaning and showing they are socially constructed, the Absurdist can tell you the same without such a dramatic showing. "Of course gender roles are created by Society and thereby changeable!" we cry. "They are a prominent elusion in Society and provide a fundamental form of social organization. They provide meaning and depth to experience." Trans activists for instance do not challenge this. In fact, by organizing the whole of their experience and action around gender, they actually infuse it with *even more* meaning. Gender remains a fundamental organizational principle of human societies, and simply challenging the categories of that organization does not challenge the organizational practice itself.

These moralists can attack Absurdism — along with its philosophical precursor Nihilism — for its amorality. Not *immorality*, mind you, for immoralists have their ethic and system[11]. Amoralism in Absurdism does not care about being iconoclast; it simply cares about maintaining a method devoid of any moral system. Camus struggles with this aspect in *The Myth*, at once stating "everything is permitted" yet also asserting this does not mean "nothing is forbidden"[12]. This is a conundrum that does not concern me — I approach this analysis as a scientist, not a lifestyle coach. Judging the morality of this-or-that action is not the purpose of the absurdist; there are courts and public opinion for that.

---

[10] For example, see Hartmann (1979) for an analysis of the relationship between Marxism and Feminism.
[11] For instance, see Camus' critique of Chestov in *The Myth* (page 34).
[12] See page 67.

Consequently, a society likely cannot exist if it is entirely comprised of absurdists. But this is of no concern; variability in nature, as I discuss later, will not allow this to happen anyway.

Therefore, attacks on the amorality of Absurdism remain largely irrelevant. Moral questions only interest us insofar as they are elusions. Moral equivalency is a central tenant of our logic: "everything is permitted" is the ultimate, dumb power of the universe. Nature still destroys all it brings into existence regardless of its behavior or function. This is not to say that Absurdism cannot guide an individual's life — it has guided mine for years. It does not require a certain class of action, only a certain kind of perspective. Absurdism is not built to tell people what to do, it exists solely to organize experience and aid perception.

Allow me to illustrate one final critique: the popular critique. Similar to the utilitarian critique, this charge is commonly levied against Absurdism by armies of undergraduate students. Absurdism is not worth your time, according to this system of thought, *not* because it is not useful. It is not worth your time because *no one cares* about it to begin with. This can be described as 'intentional intellectual myopia'. There is a large class of individuals in contemporary society (perhaps the majority) who prefer to bathe in the swamp of elusion rather than challenge it. Whenever lofty ideas about ontology or metaphysics or other philosophical pursuits are encountered, they immediately turn away. Reality for them is limited to direct (largely unconscious) experience oriented toward satiating this or that desire[13]. The questions of existence are unimportant as long as football is on — these riddles can be dealt with later. That is what churches are for when you are old.

---

[13] My conceptualization of the unconscious varies significantly from popular understanding—it is when your cognition and action are given over entirely to the Natural Machine and Indoctrinated Self. More on this in chapters 5 and 7.

Such critiques do not bother the Absurdist one bit. They are not critiques; they are data. They are elusions in action and should be treated as such. When an individual suddenly and deliberately turns away from the absurd, this is when the True Scientist pays they most attention. An entire existence can be spent describing and cataloguing variations in this turning away.

Enough of critiques; I could fill an entire volume with them. On to the business at hand.

IV) The Problem to be Examined

All scientific endeavors begin with a research question or problem. Camus began *The Myth* with the problem of suicide — namely, why one commits it. In this book the problem is your (and my) minds. How do they operate, and how can the absurdist method shed light on this process?

This book can also be characterized as an investigation into prominent themes in contemporary life. For instance, determining if the 'soul' exists. By 'soul' I do not mean that cornerstone of religion that infuses the individual with a sense of uniqueness and immortality. I mean the existence of an idiosyncratic element greater than the sum of our mental parts. Specifically, if there is a natural aspect to your cognition and personality, and if there is a social aspect as well (what Sociologists often call "identity"[14]), is there anything else? If there is something that makes you uniquely you, is this a structural aspect of your mind or is it simply the byproduct of interaction between your natural and social aspects?[15] Put bluntly: are you a meat robot running a social script or is there an additional element that makes you who you are?

This question was asked throughout the ages in one form or another, often with a certain sense of squeamishness. Most religious explorations (especially western) start from the desire that the soul exists; hardly an unbiased premise. Interestingly, some of the most religious individuals I know are also scientists. Through their work they provide example after example that the soul's existence is suspect, let alone

[14] See Stryker and Burke (2000).
[15] This is what social scientists commonly refer to as an "interaction effect". It is the statistical notion that an object is not only the sum of its parts, but also the *relationship* these parts have with one another. For instance, a white male is not simply the addition of a score for being white and a score for being male. These two elements also interact multiplicatively, where the combination of white male has a special additional score than another combination, say, white female. See Knoke et al. (2002) for further details.

immortal. Later in this text, I undertake the rather dark and dangerous orientation that the soul as we know it may not exist at all. I attempt to encounter this question from the most unbiased orientation possible (after all, who would not want to prove that the soul exists?), and to illuminate all the consequences thereafter.

Illustrations aside, these are the specific questions we seek to answer: what is the anatomy of the human mind? What are the consequences of this absurdist expedition? I examine these questions in the following order. First, I investigate the natural aspect of the human mind, what I call the *Natural Machine*. Second, I examine the socialized aspect of mind and personality, called the *Indoctrinated Self*. Next, I examine how these components of the mind interrelate. Lastly, I examine the consequences of this analysis, and the impact it has on various topics (the soul, afterlife, meaning, and everyday life).

There are already thousands of explanations on how the human mind works. I have no interest in exploring all the twists and turns in the development of cognitive theory, nor am I particularly interested in critiquing them. As I mentioned, the reasoning for this disregard is *methodological*. I avoid related works to keep my intellectual perceptions clear(er) and (somewhat) unbiased[16]. This has the added advantage of fostering intellectual innovation by finding new results independent from any pre-existing cannon of thought. My aim is to produce an original, illuminating analysis.

---

[16] These cute parentheticals are meant to call attention to the impossibility of unbiased research and the relevance of science in general. All science is influenced by the beliefs and perceptions of the scientist, no matter how strict the controls. See Latour (1988) for an excellent discussion on the social construction of science.

V) The Natural Machine

I begin my absurdist investigation of the mind with its natural aspect, what I call the *Natural Machine*. In *The Myth*, natural phenomena are often treated as external to the individual. While Camus implies the opaqueness of the natural aspects of the self when discussing "living without appeal", these ideas remain underdeveloped[17]. In this chapter, I give this topic full attention to determine its consequences for understanding the human mind.

First, let me begin with a matter of definition. What exactly do I mean by the "natural" and the "natural world"? While this definition may contrast from others (including Camus, who never actually defines it), the natural world can be thought in the broadest sense as everything outside the consciousness of a given individual. There is the self-aware, intentional aspect of the human mind and then everything else. This conceptualization not only incorporates aspects of the physical world, but also many elements commonly ascribed to the social world as well.

Allow me to set boundaries on this concept. The most obvious content it includes are the objects and processes studied under physical science. The natural includes everything from weather patterns to geology, from nuclear physics to biology, and everything in between. Additionally, the natural also includes the target of medical science; the human body. All its automatic processes and innate features fall under its purview, from organ function to skeletal structure. These are the aspects of the human form which operate and exist mostly independent of conscious direction or influence.

While the above can be included in my definition of "the natural" with little objection, my definition of this

---

[17] For instance, see Camus' discussion of the human heart on page 19 of *The Myth.*

concept also extends to human behavior. Often the purview of the social sciences and psychology, this text views individual and collective human behavior as manifestations of the same natural processes that cause blizzards and rainbows. This is not to say that both sets of phenomena are equivalent—they are simply defined as sharing the same ontology. If the world is defined by physicists as a bundle of atoms constantly in motion yet held together by various laws, my perspective merely gives the 'atom', or the most reducible element of a whole, a different *scale*[18]. All natural objects, every piece of matter in the universe, can be thought of an 'atom', or element that comprises the whole. When combined, all these pieces of the puzzle create the natural world.

Now then, it is readily accepted in physical science that particles, atoms, molecules — whatever have you — act on other units of the same and differing type. My definition of the natural merely expands this conceptualization of force in the natural world and applies it to the social world. It makes social phenomena part of natural processes. By this definition, the acting of an oxygen molecule on steel is ontologically equivalent to one person acting on another. Both are manifestations of natural force, just on different scales and with different results.

I hear the cries of protest already — "reductionism, reductionism! In seeking to challenge the utility of natural science for the explanation of human existence, all the dim-witted author does is reinforce it! This 'amoralist' is nothing but a utilitarian rationalist!". This is an understandable yet inaccurate critique. In a modern academia where Social Constructionist, Post-Modernist, Post-Structuralist, Post-Materialist, "Post" this and "Post" that run rampant, any kind of assertion that links social objects to natural processes comes under fire. Allow me to be bold: all social objects *are* natural

---

[18] I am aware that the atom is not the most reduced form of matter. It is utilized here merely as an illustration.

objects. *Yes*, social objects are constructed in the minds of men, not turtles or rocks. *Yes*, they are created using socially constructed lexicons, ideas, and frames. *But* one must look further back — where do the human minds that created all these social objects come from? What are they based upon? *Precisely those natural objects physical science occupies itself with.*

One should not, however, take this logic to the extreme; just because two things are related does not mean one is dependent on the other. This is the stumbling block that Sociobiology encounters. Just because something is naturally derived, that does not mean that it is naturally determined. Ontologically, social objects may find their origin in the naturally constructed mind, the biological basis of the brain. But once these objects are created and *distributed*, they behave according to their own logic. This is not to reify social objects — they do not drink and breathe. They do however become a social, collective product. Once distributed they are reinterpreted, changed, and disseminated by all who encounter them. They cease being connected to any biological structure, even though they may be influenced by a multitude of biological structures. The important point is, however, that these social objects had natural origins and are almost constantly reconfigured by natural objects (people), yet they are discursive and not natural forms, even though they have natural consequences.

What confusion! More evidence of the complex and contradictory nature of the natural world. Let us circle back. To this point, my definition of the natural world includes all the objects of physical and medical science, along with humans themselves and their behaviors, processes, and social structures. Some of you may already be positing another challenge to this definition:

> "What does it leave out? This appears to be a definition that defines everything; a concept that includes everything in existence. If it includes everything, then it is not defining anything,

since the whole reason why you define
something is to differentiate it from other
things!".

This is a very good critique but, yet again, it is inaccurate. It is simply a matter of perspective. "Nature" in this study — while a concept — is not defined conceptually. It is defined instead as a *perspective*, and must be understood through the framework of the absurd relationship between man and itself. The natural world then is everything external to the individual's consciousness, or the intentional thought process. Everything beyond his *willful focus*, both outside his body and within his mind, is the natural world. This is what he strives to shape and impact, and often fails at doing so (more on this later).

In sum, the 'natural' is conceptualized as what the individual strives to impact yet has no control over. The applies to both processes and objects, inanimate and human. It is everything beyond 'yourself'.

Now the absurd vision of nature comes to light. Human experience takes on the character of the lone individual standing in a dark, incoherent room, constantly ravaged by swirls of light and muddled sounds. But we are not interested in the natural world *out there*. We want to examine the natural world *in here*…inside our very minds.

This leads to the *Natural Machine*. Until now, the natural can be thought of as white noise — something man cannot understand yet desires to grasp; something incoherent yet desired. The Natural Machine on the other hand makes its home right in our head. We experience it internally, usually as a separate entity. In the following pages I first describe the Natural Machine and then discuss how it functions as a process. I close this chapter with two case studies that apply findings from this analysis and a short discussion of the consequences of this concept.

i) Describing the Natural Machine

The name of this term is intentional. The Natural Machine is the chaos and complication of Nature, yet also the constant drone of automata. Being a derivative of Nature, it is, by nature, contradictory. It is programmatic chaos with its own script that exists independently of our will and consciousness.

Some may make light of this definition and write off the Natural Machine as plagiarism of Freud's "id". Soon, they may do the same by conflating my conceptualization of the *Soul* with Freud's "ego", and the *Indoctrinated Self* with Freud's "superego". These comparisons are not surprising, yet they are also incorrect. The purpose of this study is not to create a new theoretical structure of the human mind or to develop a rehashed brand of psychotherapy. The purpose of this study is to see what Absurdism *adds* to our understanding of the mind, particularly in a world where the disjuncture between man's desires and the world's unreasonableness is becoming increasingly apparent. There is no theorizing here: the value of this analysis is not building upon one theory, but extending the absurdist methodology to the mind and examining the evidence and consequences. Doctrinal issues aside, let us first examine the qualitative aspects of the Natural Machine.

The character of the Natural Machine is varied yet surprisingly simple. I prefer to think of it as an annoying, petulant imp sitting in the corner, throwing feces and spitting phlegm whenever it does not get its way. It is a creature completely occupied with desires and satiety, and when one desire is satisfied it soon moves onto another that must be satisfied. It is, in short, the common element we share with creatures of the forest and sea.

The Natural Machine has a primary desire from which all others are apparently distilled: its *demand of recognition*. It seeks to force your consciousness to pay attention to it constantly, and to take its needs as necessary. It is a tyrant, and wants to be in command continuously. This demand is often expressed through other, more proximate demands, usually of baser inclinations. For instance, sexual gratification and gluttony are the first that come to mind for many people, but these are not necessarily the best illustrations. Perhaps the basest inclination is that studied at length by Nietzsche, the *Will to Power*[19]. The Natural Machine wants, quite simply, the one thing it can never have — to impact the natural world significantly. Such an impact would not only demand its recognition from the consciousness, but it would also, most importantly, result in some lasting change in the world beyond it. It is an amusing situation and an excellent illustration of the contradictory character of Nature. The Natural Machine's will to power is essentially an individual manifestation of nature fighting Nature as a whole.

This observation is too important to go without further explanation. The Natural Machine achieves recognition both in the individual's consciousness and the outside world by creating some sort of change. This change may (and does) take a variety of manifestations and is sought almost constantly by the Eluded. In any given situation, an individual Natural Machine will seek recognition by[20]: eliciting a laugh from a colleague; moving a table that is pushing into their stomach; relieving themselves in the bathroom; keeping the dinner bill below fifty dollars; catching a train before it departs. Notice that these examples include both social and natural behavior. These petty, everyday actions are often enacted more or less unconsciously — man feels an impulse at this second or that, some kind of desire to impact their bodies, their surroundings, or other people. These meaningless, relatively inconsequential actions —

---

[19] The concept, not the book. See Kaufman (1974) for an excellent overview of Nietzsche's thought.

[20] Recognition should not to be confused with acting in accordance with social roles, as described by Role Identity Theory (Stryker and Burke, 2000). The latter has more in common with the relationship between the Natural Machine and the Indoctrinated Self, discussed in Chapter 7.

however small — still gratify the constant demand of recognition from the Natural Machine.

Perhaps some broader examples are in order. The first that comes to mind is *Faust*[21]. His articulate and decorous appearance does not hide the commonality of his desire. Faust and the Natural Machine both demand satiation, and both experience the impossibility of this satiation. Like the Natural Machine, Faust attempts to find solace in a variety of formats. His first was intellectual development. This *seeking* is an important endeavor that should not be passed over quickly.

For many in contemporary society, satiation (commonly called 'happiness') is pursued behaviorally during their childhood and adult years. These are often enterprises aimed at acquiring some socially valued status or object through personal action. For instance, a child will attempt to win a game to satiate their blatant will to power; a teenage boy will strive to impress a girl to achieve sexual gratification; a young professional will work overtime to earn a promotion. All these actions are externally oriented, aimed at impacting the natural world and drawing a concession from it.

Only once individuals grow older will this pattern possibly change. They begin to realize the absurdity of an existence based on hopes when the future only guarantees death. Upon this realization (usually accompanied by physical decline) they sometimes strive to find *intellectual* satiation[22]. Up until this point intellectual knowledge often slants utilitarian; it is a tool for achieving this or that valued goal. But with the persistent decay of the physical form and the growing restrictions on applying the body to various tasks (along with various social restrictions, such as retirement), the satiation once achieved by actions external to the self become more elusive.

---

[21] Goethe (2008).
[22] But not always. Others will not give up this pattern of behavior so easily. An extreme example is seventy-year-olds running marathons.

Thus, the mind turns inward. Suddenly, the person is now a philosopher and intellectual, an expert in the realm of politics, literature, or whatever content they prefer. The potency lost in the body is transferred to the mind (metaphorically), and the logger and factory worker now believe themselves a Caesar or Sartre. This pursuit is all the more comforting since it requires relatively little validation from the external world. The occasional witticism in the presence of family or the polemical speech before friends is all that is required. Formal degrees do not matter. As long as speeches are sufficiently verbose and somewhat coherent, they will do. The ego is massaged, the Natural Machine confirmed, and what little crumb of momentary satiation can be extracted from the situation is realized.

It is not a requirement however that such a change happen in old age. Conditions are certainly more favorable during this season of life (retirement and cable news make the table for it), but it certainly happens in other stages of life depending on the individual. For instance, those in our society deemed as having sufficient intelligence (not to say this is empirically the case) are carted off to universities by their middle-class parents to emulate their path toward mediocrity. In the modern era, university majors and curriculum are increasingly oriented toward technical vocations valued in capitalist economies (engineering, business, accounting, chemistry). Consequently, the gross intellectualism of college studies become more and more base. Editorializing aside, the liberal arts and social science curriculums still exist (to some extent), with the apparent intention of fostering intellectual flexibility and growth in our young folk — "opening their minds" and "expanding their views" are the catchphrases that come to mind. Regardless, young people of privileged lineages are encouraged to some extent to engage in these intellectual fancies. These rather brief pursuits often live and die over the course of a semester, and rarely achieve more than the pursuits of the elderly. They often focus on challenging the elementary worldview of a student with one or two (three, tops) equally elementary worldviews from a different time or place. But as stated previously, such expeditions into nascent thinking and reflection are quite brief and entirely forgotten once the young adult enters the economy. There, knowledge is practical or it is of no merit; it serves the completion of whatever task while the rest is forgotten or decays in the dusty bookshelves of the mind.

That is if one chooses not to become a 'professional intellectual' like Faust. Here is an interesting class of people. Counting myself among its ranks, I find it completely unsurprising that Faust swung to the extreme of corporeal satiation from this pursuit of intellectual satiation. I took a sojourn from the intellectual way of life myself. Those able to stay within this this pondering climate must meet one specific criteria: they must lack imagination.

As I alluded to previously, academia is as much about politics as about knowledge. The best way to secure a career is to parrot the ideas of your contemporaries (with minor modifications); especially those on your dissertation or tenure committees. Consequently, theoretical development progresses at a snail's pace, and the demand to constantly produce 'new' (but not too new) knowledge leads to the splintering of theoretical traditions and a general incoherence in any given discipline[23]. The end result is a greater conformity of research that privileges comfort over veracity, compliance over audacity.

Such an environment is ideal for the Natural Machine. Producing articles and books that live indefinitely on the shelves of poorly circulated publications, the professional

---

[23] This is especially prevalent in the field of Sociology, the academic background of your dear author. Once dominated by macro theories that gave order to the discipline (Functionalism, Conflict Theory, Social Constructionism), the rise of Post-Modernism led to a miniaturization of theory to the socially molecular level. Now there are theories for everything from strip clubs to online chat rooms. Specializations for Sociologists also met a similar fate.

intellectual feels a confirmation of his posterity. This comfortable existence is occasionally punctuated by locking horns with his kind over various trifling details, and nothing gives the Natural Machine that strongly desired confirmation of power more than defeating an intellectual rival in the pages of a journal or at sparsely attended conferences. On top of that, this intellectual animal also takes part in that vanity fair known as college lecturing, where the loftiness of his knowledge is capable of reducing an army of undergraduates into gaping mouths and drool-soaked desks. What a beautiful, vain life, truly capable of embodying a great quote: "The ass arrived, beautiful and most brave" [24].

I apologize for the length of this polemic. It is not only therapeutic for me in my exile from the Ivory Tower, but it is also necessary to foster understanding of Faust's environment. What self-respecting creature, what man with any ounce of creativity or free thinking could endure such conditions! Faust attempted to feed himself on the *diversity* of thought, not its profundity. I did so as well. Over the course of his career, he tackles everything from medicine to law, satiating his desire for intellectual conquest momentarily, until he understands a topic adequately. Then it is off to the next thing. When we first encounter him, he has just finished his journey across all scientific knowledge. The elation of his victory is absent; there is only frustration and disappointment.

Why is he in such a disposed state? Because he did not find what he sought. Faust wanted the keys to the natural world and they alluded him. Deploying science, magic, religion; none of the methods mattered, the result was always the same. The *allusion* of Natural Truth led him to *elude* himself with Gretchen and carnal sentiments. This is the conclusion so many 'free spirits' find themselves fulfilling. Faust is an innocent, he wants to know. He does not have the strength however to realize that, as the Absurdist says, we can

---

[24] See Nietzsche (1989: 15).

never know. He runs from the paucity of the intellectual to the savagery of the corporeal.

And so, Faust traverses the different manifestations of the Natural Machine. These different paths can indeed appear highly discordant; what do the efforts of the intellectual have to do with those of the construction worker? But it is only *form* that is different here, not function. In the end, the Natural Machine endlessly seeks its confirmation, and in doing so runs man's body and mind into the dirt.

I will refrain from more examples regarding the quality of the Natural Machine; I have assaulted your ears enough. Instead, let us examine the *process* of the natural aspect of ourselves.

ii) The Process of the Natural Machine

When I talk about *process*, I am specifically concerned with how the Natural Machine behaves and actuates. As previously mentioned, it is the marriage of chaos and calculation; randomness and control. Such characteristics are contradictory, and thus reflective of its natural origins.

Chaos and Order are not as discordant as one may think. If the core tenants of statistical theory such as normality and the central limit theorem are believed[25], then randomness itself follows a pattern that is predictable. While such theorizations clearly illuminate man's "nostalgia" as Camus calls it[26], and the efficacy of such instruments can be called into question[27], they do present an interesting paradox: chaos is predictably chaotic. Something that is completely

---

[25] And these are, indeed, significant assumptions regarding the distribution of data and the randomness of error. See Knoke et al. (2002) for an overview of these topics.

[26] Statistical theory is an excellent illustration of man's desire to understand and control the natural. The unpredictability of the natural world is reduced to an error term in an equation and thereby 'controlled'.

[27] For example, it is not unusual for the R^2 value (the score that shows the amount of variation in a population that a regression model explains) to be quite low. Such inconveniences are often overlooked in academic journals.

random is not *completely* random, because it can always be counted on to be completely random.

Perhaps an example is in order. Waves on a beach, when examined *closely*, are all unique and different. There is an immeasurable amount of water molecules undulating and cascading, and the arrangement of these small chunks of matter is influenced by an immense number of confounding variables (season, tide, moon phase, temperature, turbidity, etc.). But the waves still come. Save a massive change in environment (which has happened and will happen in the future; Nature never allows things to be too predictable), the randomness of the rate and appearance of these waves will not cease. Put simply, they are reliably unreliable.

Now let us extend this logic to the Natural Machine living inside our minds. For many, it dictates a significant majority of their cognition. It can be thought of as the hand behind the camera of what Heidigger calls "the intention"[28]. It moves our perception from this object to that, from one task to the next, much like how one aims a flashlight at various points in a dark room. Each time something new is revealed, but the focus of our mind is also changed. Previous objects lose their focus and over time may be forgotten. It is this movement from object to object that describes the primary function of the Natural Machine.

This movement is different from person to person regarding its *Frequency*, *Randomness*, and *Capacity* to be influenced[29]. Variability in these attributes can logically be innate, shaped by the individual, or their surroundings. I examine each variable in turn.

---

[28] Camus provides an excellent description of this concept in *The Myth*; see page 43.

[29] This is not an exhaustive list of variability in the Natural Machine. For example, it can also vary by level of activity, stamina, and other attributes.

When it comes to *Frequency*, some of us experience changes in thought more often than others[30]. If this occurs with enough regularity, it is pathologized by the medical institution as Attention Deficit Hyperactivity Disorder or whatever else. Possessing a 'jumpy' Natural Machine is not necessarily a curse however. Mine is extremely active, and my life is not reduced to constant distraction managed by pills. Those of us with active Natural Machines, while often more distracted, have a front row seat to the operation of the natural world. We *feel* it, we *experience* it all the more profoundly, because the natural aspect of our mind illustrates it to us simply by its movement.

Natural Machines also vary by *Randomness*. By this I mean the *quality* of topics the mind jumps to. While one Natural Machine may have a high frequency of movement between topics, many of these topics may correspond to the same task, causing this Machine to have low randomness. Take for example an office work situation. I am compiling a project on the rate of economic growth in whatever state, and there are a variety of tasks necessary to complete this report. While the elements of this task may be socially determined (gathering data, cleaning data, conducting statistical tests, interpreting results, creating a document, etc.), and their progression meant to follow a logical order, my Natural Machine can change the game. For instance, it can spur me to run statistical models immediately after I receive the data, forsaking data cleaning. It can dig into my memory and use learned information about methodology to complicate what specific technique should be used. It can also confound matters by taking anxiety in one area of life (say my child's performance at school), and transfer that anxiety into this

---

[30] It is important to note here that changes in perception are not entirely influenced by the Natural Machine—later chapters show the complexity of the human cognitive process. At this point, we are merely observing how this part of the mind changes our perception.

project ("am I doing this right? I should check it again and again and again...").

This aspect of randomness in a task should be clearly understood within the universe of absurd thought. Man's confrontation with an unreasonable and contradictory natural world causes anxiety and strain. This in turn leads almost all men to attempt to elude it. This is a function of the individual's Natural Machine acting against the natural world. Applied to my example, the necessity of completing a task correctly and in a timely fashion induces strain in my Natural Machine. It would prefer to not have anything imposed on it (thus having free reign over the natural world), and when forced to perform something, it often wants to complete it as quickly as possible. This completion both relieves anxiety and allows confirmation of itself through a demonstration of power. Therefore, my Natural Machine strives to complete the task rapidly while avoiding any negative social consequences that may challenge my feeling of impact (such as errors in the report). This relieves anxiety from the world demanding something of me and induces confirmation in my Natural Machine for achieving some impact on this world. It is important to understand that there are other processes occurring in this example involving the Indoctrinated Self. These will be discussed later.

I see an objection looming on the horizon — "what about those who are lazy? What about the dropout or the ritualist[31], who refuse to engage in as many socially necessary tasks as possible or simply zombie though what is required to earn a paycheck?". My response is twofold. First, the activity of the Natural Machine is *variable* in all its aspects; there is no universal constant for how it should behave or the *specific* quality it should take. Second, and once again, this part of the analysis is solely concerned with the Natural Machine. The relationship between the Machine and the Indoctrinated Self is

---

[31] See Merton (1938) for an explanation of this term.

a complex one which certainly structures the behavior of the lazy and destitute in society. This complex interaction is examined in Chapter 7.

Of course, randomness can also involve the Natural Machine focusing our consciousness or projecting memories from areas completely unrelated to the given task. For instance, at the moment of this writing, Toto's *Africa* is playing in my head. Why? I do not know; it just happened. This aspect of the Natural Machine is the most illustrative of how it is a *natural* phenomenon. While you and Society may be able to *influence* it, to *push* it in one direction *for a time*, the Natural Machine often simply does what the Natural Machine wants, spawning this or that cognition it demands. This is such an integral aspect of the human experience yet few ever realize it, and it is often defined as an aspect of personality in medical and clinical establishments.

But I assert it is something *different*. I can build walls around my intention and *force* it to put words on these pages, but my Natural Machine is almost constantly revolting. My mind briefly jumps to whether or not I locked my house door, to the lottery jackpot tonight, to the whole list of 'things that need to be done' today. Then it also just spaces out. This tension between willful action and automatic action is the absurd condition unfolding in the mind.

Many give themselves over entirely to the Natural Machine, especially outside structured social settings (work, religious ceremonies, group projects, etc.). Unrestricted, it often engages in daydreaming and thoughts about whatever factor is limiting its free exercise at the moment. There is also that abominable curse of *sleep*, where the body paralyzes itself and the Natural Machine runs wild, engaging in all sorts of fantasies and anxieties. Once again, these cognitions may be influenced or limited by the social, but they tend to act as if they had a 'life of their own'[32].

These situations are when the human is least human, and it is in these conditions that many people spend a majority of their lives. This is the entire reason why we have the concept *focusing* — it is a specific activity that pulls the Natural Mind out of the *flow*[33] of its daily routine. But as Camus illustrates, everything pushes man forward and away from contemplation[34]. As I discuss later, Society tends to be structured to keep man in this flow of automata, discouraging any reflection by an aware individual[35]. The importance of work in western societies, the engrossing character of our modern pastimes (sports, video games, films, etc.); these are just a few examples of how contemporary life discourages reflection and encourages relatively unconscious experience, either passively (watching television) or actively (playing soccer or cards).

The Natural Machine pushes us forward as well. Entirely engrossed with its quest to impact the natural world, it seeks to accelerate the experience of time and jam in more opportunities for confirmation. Before he knows it, our once valiant conqueror is now an old man in a nursing home. "How did this happen? Time flies by so fast!" — these are the common refrains. By limiting consciousness from reflection and assaulting it with a constant flurry of hopes and demands, the Natural Machine slowly yet surely tucks man into his grave.

To sum up, randomness, like frequency, is a variable property of the Natural Machine that may be influenced by the individual and society but cannot be fully controlled. This

---

[32] A good example of the independence of cognition is Nietzsche's description of the philosopher, "who is struck by his own thoughts as from outside..." (1989: 230).
[33] See Csíkszentmihályi (1975) for a study on this concept.
[34] See page 58 in *The Myth* for a discussion of this process.
[35] This cognitive process is complex and discussed in Chapters 6 and 7. It involves successful coordination between the natural and social aspects of the self.

brings us to the last characteristic of the Natural Machine I will examine: its *Capacity to be controlled.*

"What?! An apparent contradiction! You just wrote at length about the Natural Machine, depicting it as a wily beast dominating our lives. But now you swing back and say it has a collar and leash?!". Of course I did. Nature is contradictory. Nothing is permanent or free from change, especially the experience of the absurd condition which requires a person to *willfully refuse* elusion. Do not worry, I am not selling you those poppies I decried in the previous chapter. There is no attempt here to soothe and console. I am merely exploring many sides of the same process.

Yes, like a dog, the Natural Machine can be broken. But this is a matter of *extent* — no dog is perfectly trained, nor can it be since it is a creature of Nature. Perhaps the most significant function of the Indoctrinated Self is its constant desire to steer the Natural Machine and bring its behavior in line with socialized expectations. This thought is by no means new, and once again smacks of Freud. It will be unpacked fully in the following chapters.

Perhaps the more interesting limitation placed on the Natural Machine is from the natural world. I am not assigning consciousness to the matter and phenomenon of the universe. What I am doing is treating the natural world as a *process*; specifically a process with significant consequences. During the interaction of a single Natural Machine with the natural world, the absurd condition is played out in naked clarity.

As previously mentioned, this takes the form of an individual distillation of the natural assaulting another *specific* element of the natural. This is the most common manifestation of this process. More rarely, it can also be an individual piece of the natural revolting against the natural world as a whole. Examples of the former range from a child pushing rocks to debates between political candidates, while the latter includes actions that upend the fundamental assumptions of contemporary life, such as suicide. This is why Camus' study of suicide in *The Myth* is so instructive. This one act is loaded with so many consequences, so much social meaning, that it questions the core elusions of society and reveals the fundamental strain between the individual and the world.

I do not intend to discuss the most common manifestation of this natural versus natural dynamic at great length. The most illustrative examples happen between individuals. These situations are mediated by social meanings and objects (language, topics, norms, etc.), and are touched upon in later chapters. I can however examine how the individual Natural Machine confronts inanimate manifestations of the natural world, such as its objects (mountains, lakes) and its processes (weather, reproduction).

The results of these types of analyses produce no profound results. Camus states that the sterility of action or thought are often indicative of the absurd condition, and investigations on this topic are indeed sterile. A Natural Machine can engage a piece of Nature and attempt to bend it to their will (metalworking or flight for instance), and it can also graft notions onto it and incorporate Nature into a system of meaning, thereby giving the (false) impression that it is controlled or managed. These examples are often the purview of physical science and, consequently, allow a rather easy opportunity to illustrate the limits of the Natural Machine in shaping and explaining the natural world.

As previously mentioned, anything measured by science contains *error*, and this error itself is evidence of a natural world that defies attempts at being controlled and understood. In the case of our examples, there are a whole multitude of confounding effects in the world that can cause things to 'break', 'fall apart', or act 'unexpectedly'. In a word, *accidents*. Metal can shear and split when exposed to a variety of environments, conditions, and forces during its formulation and use. Elements can follow a system in a lab only to change their behavior in the ocean. The pure amount of these possible confounding effects is beyond human comprehension, which is why accidents *still happen*.

Perhaps the most illustrative example of these 'accidents' is flight. Aircraft are developed in specific environments and under very restrictive assumptions. Scientists create equations and graphs to convince themselves that these assumptions are important and robust enough to resist the confounding effects of Nature *that they can think of*. But outside of the laboratory and factory (and even within them — no matter how hard engineers attempt to standardize there are always anomalies and 'problems' in production), Nature routinely ignores the human math and human logic meant to predict and control it. What is the result? Planes crash, for a multitude of reasons. Man may be able to shape the type and frequency of these events, but he cannot prevent them. The limitations of the individual Natural Machine, desiring so profoundly to control just one sliver of the natural world, come to light again and again.

The end result is not only the frustration of the Natural Machine, but also the *shaping of its efforts* by the natural world. It seems highly unlikely to me that any Natural Machine could endure an activity with a high probability of failure for very long (unless failure is redefined as success, but even then this is unlikely). Failure after failure, the natural world pats the conqueror on the head, and helps nudge him toward something easier. Why invade Rome when Hispania will do? Forget mastering black holes and dying stars; here…dissect a frog.

Remember that Natural Machines vary however. They must, being creations of the natural, and there are some that deliberately seek out these adventures where failure is all but certain. Any success, no matter how small, is defined as a mountain. It raises our knowledge to new heights…supposedly. The absurdity of these efforts is readily apparent and they speak to the creativity of elusion. In western societies, where the value of endeavors are so often defined by *results*, and *significant* results at that (whatever those are), the extension of life by six months with a new cancer drug is cause for celebration. Never mind the *quality* of life in those six months (usually rather poor), but this result, however minute, is still held as significant.

If all else fails, the individual's endeavor can always be included as part of some general accumulation of knowledge. It is another 'step forward' in solving a problem that cannot be solved. For example, take our illustration of 'curing' cancer. What scientists are really interested in is curing death, and battling cancer is just one manifestation of this struggle. The scientist's contribution still has *some* impact and serves as a stepping stone to greater enlightenment or solving whatever paradox. But people still die, Nature still wins, and the scientist still loses.

This is enough discussion on the process of the Natural Machine for now. This topic will be explored further in coming chapters. Before moving on to examine the companion of the Natural Machine — the *Indoctrinated Self* — I illustrate these findings about the process and quality of the Natural Machine in two case studies. The first examines an *ideal type* of person with an extremely active, random, and uncontrolled Natural Machine. The second examines an interesting process of the Natural Machine, one arguably necessary for its continued existence.

iii) Case Studies of the Natural Machine: The Tyrant

When contemplating the type of person to represent the findings in this chapter, my mind immediately swung to the "Conqueror" vignette in *The Myth*[36]. I am not entirely sure why. Camus describes a man who is extensively self-aware both of himself and his state in society. This reflectiveness is anything but a characteristic of a man dominated by the

---

[36] See page 84.

Natural Machine. The Conqueror I envision is more of a *slave* dressed in king's clothing, a man with the outward appearance of being all powerful and domineering, yet internally is enchained by his passions. This is what I call the *Tyrant.*

The Tyrant is not a man of sensibility or cultivation. He does not grow or develop. He thinks of himself as ready-made, delivered to this planet in his current state, as if dropped from the moon. His past is completely forgotten, except those mental trophies he keeps around to occasionally remind himself of his greatness. They do not satisfy for long, however. He is ceaselessly driven by a painful compulsion to continue his 'success'; to experience consistently greater achievement. Society aids him in this lost quest, for capitalist economics are based upon the same principle.

While tyrannical with others, he is above all a tyrant of the self. There is constant pain and anxiety churning in his mind; constant scheming to control the outcomes of his actions and to parry the actions of others. It is often the first solution which appears in his mind that he follows. He does not believe in collaboration in his own mind or with others. His initial solution is often heavy-handed and domineering, spawning from his zero-sum logic. This is befitting to his type. He is a man of *action* above all else, and time spent in contemplation or planning is time wasted. One cannot accumulate more power or wealth in the philosopher's armchair, according to him.

His quest is indeed lost, but he does not dwell on this. His cognition is entirely fixed on the task at hand, often necessary in his mind for achieving some overarching goal. This goal is usually vague and continuous, and surprisingly little effort is expended in developing it. Like the Marxist, entirely consumed with understanding the *now* and with defeating his enemies in the present, there is a surprising lack of contemplation about the future he desires. This is fine however, for also like the Marxist, he does not want the struggle to end.

It is this struggle that breathes life into him. It is something he loves and he hates. When in the throes of battle, straining with all his might to achieve his goal, it is agonizing. He wishes to cast it off, cursing that such difficulty should ever exist. He demands everything be easy and readily apparent, that all opposition crumble before him. But it never does, and that is fine. For when he is not in the struggle, when the world conforms in those brief moments according to his mandates, he is *empty*. He senses the sterility of existence, the lack of depth. A life characterized by constant striving demands to strive. It is in these moments between actions when he is the most vulnerable and savage. Vulnerable because he loses himself; the man accustomed to constant movement becomes a temporarily paraplegic. Savage because he will do anything to get his legs back.

At this moment you may desire a concrete example. The options are bountiful. Most of the 'great' figures of history fall under this category, from all corners of the moralistic universe. There are 'honorable' men and 'evil' men, men of letters and men of warfare. They all hold in common a single thing — an insatiable desire *not to think*. Not about their own little goals or strivings, no matter how grandly they may construct them in their minds. They simply want to not think about *anything else*.

It is rather fortunate I am writing this text in the late teens of the twenty-first century, for one of the individuals most emblematic of this mental climate is putting on a magnificent show — Donald Trump. His is a character that comes by maybe once in a half century, a perfect storm of an excessively strong and unbalanced Natural Machine coupled with a fantastic turn of social arrangements leading to his rise. Hitler was most likely the last of this type[37].

Trump is fascinating due to the blind power of his Natural Machine. It does not apparently care about anyone else, and any affection shown to others appears self-serving. Alarmed by the cool hand of death inching closer and closer daily, thoughts at this man's time of life often turn to *legacy*. His support of his children can be construed as signifying their place in this legacy. But this legacy is his own; it has impact beyond his lifetime and his children are central to it. That longing for permanence, denied to us physically so we compensate socially, can lead even the most tyrannical of tyrants to bestow gifts and favor upon those they deem instrumental to its establishment and continuity.

His actions are quick and decisive. There is no deliberation, or if there is it is rendered as brief as possible. It is widely known that he favors television over reading, and that his interest is lost after mere moments during briefings with all their troublesome details[38]. Planning and understanding are not in his mind's ecology. He already knows all he needs to know. *Action* is the only pursuit he is made for.

Examining his political pursuits, the topics appear erratic and ununified[39]. There is immigration, tax reform, healthcare reform, infrastructure reform, net neutrality, sabotaging rivals' corporate mergers, the threat of a couple nuclear wars, so on and so forth. While it is certainly not uncommon for political figures to pursue multiple policies

---

[37] This is in no way meant to imply a moral judgement; this book is written outside the confines of standard western morality. This section is merely discussing the existence and behavior of a type, regardless of the moral character of their actions.

[38] For reporting on Trump's preference for television and aversion to reading, see Parker and Costa (2017) and Rosenwald (2018), respectively. For an example of his attention span, see Pasha-Robinson (2017).

[39] This is an interesting characteristic of American conservatism in general. The marriage of social and economic conservatives appears more like a mixture of oil and water than anything else, and frequent clashes are now commonplace since the early 2000s.

simultaneously, the media narrative, which he seeks to dominate, shifts almost daily in response to this or that insult, this or that threat. Thanks to his social position and the growth of technology, he is a man capable of influencing the world in a way possibly unheard of…at least since Hitler. But this is all momentary — his attacks and ramblings change by the day; by the hour even. The natural world never lets anything stick for long, especially on the national stage, and the natural process within him, his Natural Machine, pushes him onward to a new conspiracy or tirade with each rise of the sun.

In sum, Trump is a gift to philosophers everywhere. It is rare to come across such a specimen so disinterested with social norms and propriety, so blindly vain yet in such a powerful and public position. He embodies many of the most obvious aspects of the active Natural Machine — its effectiveness at skirting control, within the mind and without; the endless need for confirmation and impact on the world; the high frequency of consciousness shifting from object to object; the randomness of pursuits united by self-aggrandizement. Trump is, put simply, not a man per se, but a Natural Machine running with as little restraint as possible in modern society.

But tyrants of the mind need not always be 'evil', whatever your moral compass. There are some Society deems 'good'; as making 'significant contributions' to the wellbeing of humanity. These are the people lionized in high school textbooks — Ghandi, Martin Luther King Jr., etc. To counter the raw actionable impulse of Trump, I will not discuss the leaders of social movements or religions here. Their plane of action is still the material world. Perhaps what is most instructive is an example of how a powerful Natural Machine can be strongly oriented toward *contemplation*, mental action not physical action.

Once again, the options are manifold. To further illustrate the moral relativity of the type, I choose someone fundamental to my intellectual development, Friedrich Nietzsche.

Nietzsche illustrates the power of a Natural Machine denied material options for expression. Chronically ill for most his life and forced to retire in his mid-thirties, his was not a life punctuated with a grandiose military career (he was an orderly in the Franco-Prussian War) nor was he a captain of industry. Preeminently brilliant (he became Chair of Classical Philology at the University of Basel at age twenty-four), his academic career was cut short due to infirmity and his rejection of intellectual conformity. Languishing in the Alps and writing in solitude, stricken with chronic headaches and digestive problems, he produced some of the most significant thoughts in western philosophy prior to his death in 1900[40].

Nietzsche's life was one of chronic pain and disappointment when measured by common standards. His writings were almost entirely ignored prior to his death and were distorted and misunderstood in posterity. But it is the *intellectual tyrant* we are interested in here, not a legacy, and it is instructive to see how natural and social adversity impacted the man.

Naturally, Nietzsche's physical form was in almost constant chaos. Yet while his body failed him, the natural aspect in his mind would not rest. Nietzsche's Natural Machine was so desperate to understand, so engrossed with overcoming the absurd condition of human existence, that it drove him to produce a library's worth of notebooks and to publish volumes of text. In Nietzsche's case, his Natural Machine's desire to understand and dominate the world of ideas eclipsed the natural world's insistence that he rile in agony and social obscurity. He is a magnificent example for us all.

---

[40] For an excellent biography of Nietzsche, see Kaufmann (1974).

In sum, these examples of the Natural Machine illustrate that its thirst for domination, confirmation, and control can adopt a variety of manifestations. These were just two examples; there are endless combinations depending on individual, natural, and historical circumstances. The direction an individual takes is often, in our individualist reductionist society, described *instead* as a matter of *talent* with perhaps a light mention of opportunity. Defined as the innate essence in a man causing him to perform one task better than others, talent is often reduced to an accessory of a person. It is noted, and in some circumstances celebrated[41], yet in the average man glossed over. The work of Society must be done, and your penchant for dabbling in painting or piano is of less consequence than your ability as an accountant.

talent takes on a new meaning in this analysis. It speaks to the variation in Natural Machines in society, where some display more skill at this or that, or are more inclined to certain types of endeavors. When viewed from this perspective, it is more a matter of *focus* than talent, where the inclinations of the Natural Machine coupled with opportunities for exercising those inclinations determine where it shifts its dominating gaze. Taken in combination with other variables (frequency, randomness, controllability, etc.), the orientation and actions of the Natural Machine are shown to be far more complex than a simple talent one is born with. This is the power of the absurdist methodology — peeling away the elusions and simple assumptions behind something to reveal its manifold complexity. Absurdism directs our gaze toward complexity when our mind and society want to turn away. It is the destroyer of simplicity and complacency.

One can argue this brief analysis of characters amounted to nothing more than me putting ideas into historical figure's heads and attaching intent to actions I could

---

[41] For instance, in the case of professional sports or arts.

never possibly know. This is not an unreasonable critique, yet it misses the point of this exercise. We are discussing *ideal types* here with the aid of history. Human beings, being creatures of Nature, are dynamic and contradictory. They will never fit perfectly into any category. The purpose of this analysis is to show the operation of this type of Natural Machine that, regardless of intent or content, has a similar *character*.

In the next example, we look at a process of the Natural Machine that impacts the very foundation of our life experience.

iv) Case Studies of the Natural Machine: Memory

Memory is cruel. It is a thief, or at best a con artist. Supposedly functioning as the catalogue of our lives, it is far from an empirical history. Pages are tattered and missing. Print is smudged, crossed out and written over. Sometimes it outright lies. In our brief examination of this natural process, I will discuss two aspects of memory using the absurd methodology—recollection and forgetting.

Recollecting a memory is not recollection per se; we are not remembering what happened. We are instead remembering a *perspective* of what happened — ours — tampered with the Natural Machine's paintbrush. It is a combination of myopia and art, presenting the past from our eyes only with a growing list of distortions and artistic liberties.

If current science is believed, every time we strike a deal with that natural process and recall something another element of our past is distorted or forgotten[42]. This is most evident during 'eye-witness' testimony in legal trials. The term 'eye-witness' is indeed telling—the court relies on a particular perspective of an incident. This perspective involves recollection that transforms the past which is

---

[42] Bernstein and Loftus (2009).

impacted by a variety of confounding effects[43]. Suddenly the 'facts' of the case become manifold and contradictory. We should not be surprised. If there is any way to characterize the natural process, it is its inclination toward complexity and variation, not only in the material world, but also the world of ideas.

This process of recollection is more 'unjust' than simply forgetting. At least with forgetting we often do not remember what we forgot, saving us grief in the process. With recollection, we are left with memories, but these are memories that we *know* not to be true. The Natural Machine does its work with them; it reinterprets our past to be in line with the 'reality' it wants to convey. It does not care about accuracy; just consistency. We are left with a photo album where the events are the same but the location and the company change. And we can never get it back.

This analysis reinforces the importance of Camus' notion of freedom — the free man lives without nostalgia of the past nor hope for the future. His plane of existence is solely the present. When it comes to nostalgia, I know I am not the man I remember. My recollection of the past is not what 'really happened', it is distorted to support some narrative in either a positive or negative way. My memory reinvents my failures into conquests, or reinterprets moments of elation into things I should be ashamed of. As I discuss in the next chapter, the reinventive capacity of memory is often a co-venture between the Natural Machine and Indoctrinated Self. What we remember is not only distorted by the Natural Machine to fulfill some narrative enabling its confirmation in our minds, but it can also be changed to reinforce some moral mandate ("I shouldn't have done that; I'm so ashamed; etc). The end result, however, is the same. We progressively lose

---

[43] See Wells and Olson (2003) for an examination of the factors that impact they accuracy of eyewitness accounts.

'what really happened' with each recollection, and we forget who we really were in that moment.

Recollection is often uncontrollable. In any given situation, my Natural Machine digs into the collapsed bookshelves of my memory and fires off a mental vignette of something in my distorted past. This is similar to the *Frequency* and *Randomness* aspects of the Natural Machine discussed earlier, but in this case solely focused on memory. I am driving my car to work, and all the sudden my thoughts are assaulted with a scene from a television show I saw a year ago. I do not know why it happened, but it did[44]. When I am eating out, I am all the sudden reminded of an Italian restaurant I visited as a child. These two examples were chosen deliberately — one is keyed and the other is not.

Often, recollection is characterized as being in response to some stimulus in our environment. In the latter example above, I was eating dinner in a restaurant, so my recollection of a different restaurant at a different time and place was at least superficially connected to my present state. But these stimulus/response perspectives drain the randomness and agency from the Natural Machine. They give its behavior *depth* as Camus says; they assign a *reason* to the Natural Machine's actions. "There must be a reason for everything, right"? Except in the natural world, where reason is as foreign to it as reality. The compliance of the natural world in following a manmade framework *partially* and *up to a point* should not be mistaken for reason, especially when it ultimately contradicts itself[45]. As the first example above demonstrates, there does not have to be any obvious reason (or any reason at all) for a memory to fire in our mind. The Natural Machine does not seek our permission; it *just does*.

---

[44] Memories of mass produced social objects such as television shows or music serve a very important social function. They are lenses that project meaning onto our current situations or lives as a whole. For instance, they can infuse our present with morality by confirming our current actions or condemning them.

[45] This is meant to be reflective of Camus' "notion of limit". See page 36 in *The Myth*.

That said, recollection is also selective. The Natural Machine does not consistently produce memories at random even though it may for a period of time. As a product of Nature, it is contradictory and can often dredge up memories repetitively. This is not a reversal to the above argument; I do not mean to state that all selective memories are in response to a stimulus in the environment (although some certainly are). The Natural Machine can fire memories into our consciousness not at random yet also not in response to the outside world.

For instance, right now my Natural Machine is recollecting the guinea pig I had while a sophomore at university. There is no obvious external stimuli in my environment to induce this memory; I am sitting in a darkened basement staring at a bright screen. Now my mind transitions to the name of the guinea pig — Shakespeare — and then to the meerkat from a nature documentary he was named after. Now it is jumping to a commercial for an animated movie I saw with some animal that looked like a meerkat but was not. In this instance, there is a memory precipitated at random and then a series of other recollections with some logical tie to the initial one. Memories abide by the same logic in this case as the Natural Machine's overall behavior — it can be conditioned or 'trained' to move in one direction, but there is also a significant element of randomness and agency that it unavoidably demonstrates.

Memory and recollection also steal the present from us. This is the aspect of memory that troubles me the most. Reflective of the Natural Machine's logic, my mind will occasionally be torn from the moment and transported to a fabricated past. At one moment, I am observing the "dumb show"[46] of a man infusing his day with meaning at a *Starbucks* — say, engaging in a political debate with a friend — and then, all the sudden, I am back under the hot sun of my

---

[46] See page 15 in *The Myth*.

childhood in Texas. How this happens I do not know, and it requires effort to recollect what I was doing previously. This here is the trick — one recollection breeds another. Memory steals the present from me, soaking up what precious time I have in the here and now to fill my head with dreams and fantasies, and the only way I can get back to that reality is by inducing another recollection of my state prior to such a rude interruption. Of course, this recollection of what I was doing will not be *exactly* what I was doing or thinking previously due to the distortion inherent in the recollection process. That exact moment is lost to me forever.

Recollection is thus the most basic and innate of elusions. Our minds are structured specifically to elude ourselves, and we cannot control this. The Natural Machine breaks our perception and consciousness almost at will and floods thought with frivolity. It takes significant effort and focus to maintain some shred of autonomy during these moments; to *analyze* what my own mind is doing to me against my will. Still, as creatures of Nature it is impossible for us to be consistent, and I find my consciousness all too commonly being hijacked by my primitive, petulant self.

Enough on recollection. Allow me a few words on *forgetting*. Recollection steals our past and present and shapes it into a fantasy; it is a con artist selling us snake oil. Forgetting simply takes a past episode by robbery. I do not know what is more tragic for you, being forced to relive a lie or not being able to relive anything at all, but I do know forgetting is one of the Natural Machine's most powerful mechanisms.

Can you remember every failure in life? Can you remember every time you went up against Nature, either inanimate or social, and lost? Of course not. Doing so would flood your cognition with boundless evidence of the absurd; it would make elusion impossible. The best way to enable elusion is to simply forget one of the terms required for the absurd relationship to exist at all. That is what forgetting does.

In its ceaseless striving for confirmation, for impacting the world, the Natural Machine does not tolerate failure. Coincidentally much is forgotten. "But that's not so!" you may yell. "I can remember plenty of times when I've failed!". Three observations on this contention. First, you remember them only after intentional effort to recall them. Second, these recollections are not, once again, the actual events that happened. And third, these recollections are often reinterpreted and infused with some sort of meaning. While the Natural Machine cannot tolerate failure, that does not mean it does not have a use for it. Failure allows the Natural Machine to justify its current orientation of action, along with reminding you what directions failed in the past. It is a learning tool for the Natural Machine, a way to avoid future loss. But we should not overstate the extent to which this happens—failure is something to be avoided.

That is, unless failure is desired. Supporting the contradictory character of Nature, there is nothing that stops the Natural Machine from setting failure as a goal. This is the favorite pastime of the depressed. By failing *consistently*, the Natural Machine seeks to impart a constant state on a dynamic world. The man incapable of getting up in the morning, incapable of putting on his shoes and going to work, incapable of performing the litany of small actions our society demands on a daily basis—this man aligns his behavior to achieve his goal. He seeks the consistency of chronic disappointment, so much so that when something deemed good occasionally happens to him, he rushes to minimize it or redefine it negatively—"Yes I got a new job, but now I have so much more responsibility!" or my favorite, "Yes, I had a good date, but she will never understand me, plus her teeth are too big!".

These findings are the consequences of free thought. We see the walls of our cell all the more clearly and understand the construction of our prison to the brick. Does it matter that we have such vision? That we can see the tyranny of the natural so clearly, and feel it so profoundly? These are explorations for a later chapter.

v) Consequences

This introduction and analysis of the Natural Machine holds many significant consequences. It reveals how much our daily lives are dominated by this chaotic natural process. It also shows the variability and contradiction there is in this process as well. But the most profound consequence of the Natural Machine is the recognition it forces from us that we are not as exceptional as we want to believe. The basic structure of our cognition has more in common with the inchworm than any deity. This insight has consequences that extend to humanity's social evolution, where history can be interpreted as the constant striving of mankind to prove to itself that it is something different and *better* than all other life forms on this planet. This analysis shows that even though we possess greater knowledge than the cat or dog, the basic cognitive *process* of our thought brings us closer to Nature than any attempt to tear us apart. Content aside, we have far more in common with the ant than differences.

The objections to this analysis are clear: it strips agency from the individual and presents them as nothing more than a programmatic, chaotic robot. These cries of 'Reductionism' were addressed when I discussed physical science in the first chapter. The Natural Machine, while powerful, is not the entirety of man himself. It is one piece of his mental puzzle, but not the only piece. In the next chapter, we examine the *social aspect* of the human mind with the absurdist methodology.

VI) The Indoctrinated Self

There is another side to our minds that harkens from an (apparently) different source. It is commonly referred to as the "conscious" in popular society, or the "superego" in Freudian circles. If the Natural Machine represents the chaotic tyranny of Nature, this force represents the restraint of Society. This *Indoctrinated Self* as I call it is the sometimes adversary, sometimes ally of the natural aspect in ourselves.

This chapter examines this social influence over our minds. I do so by explaining its *quality* and its *process*. I conclude this chapter with a few illustrations on how this process behaves. First, however, it is important to include some background concerning the process of installing the Indoctrinated Self in the person, and the characteristics of the society imprinted in the person. It is important to note that most of this analysis is conducted without considering the Indoctrinated Self's relationship with the Natural Machine, which I discuss later. Before we examine relationships, we must first understand the *terms* of those relationships.

i) Indoctrination and Society

The *quality* of the Indoctrinated Self can be conceptualized as the individual's society cohabitating in their mind. Easy enough. I hear two questions already: "Isn't this simply Freud's superego?" and "Why call it the 'Indoctrinated' Self? Why not the *Socialized* Self?". It is important to address each of these objections in turn as they will aid in revealing the quality of this concept.

First, Freud. My answer to this critique is identical to the previous charge levelled against the Natural Machine. I do not care about Freud. If some of my explanation here happens to overlap with his work, then good on him; he developed something somewhat useful. If it runs contrary, then all the better. To remind, this analysis cares only about the application of the absurdist methodology to the human mind. It is an *inductive enterprise*; the less I know of a competing theory the better. The intention here is not to 'win' or disprove this or that notion — if I wanted to do that I would stay in academia. The intent is merely to follow Camus' method to its fullest extent, and to consider what it reveals. I leave it up to the reader to make whatever determination they like regarding its utility for understanding.

Second, this idea of the 'Socialized' versus the 'Indoctrinated' Self. The choice of my language is intentional — it means to draw more attention to the involuntary nature of this process. It is like the poison poured into King Hamlet's ear, it is done while *sleeping*. Not in the clinical sense of course, but in the *developmental*. The mandates, norms, and beliefs of society are forced into our minds before we can organize any defense. They set up a creature in our heads, jerking us this way and that, much as the Natural Machine does. It is this involuntary process that destroys the innocence of the newborn mind that I examine first.

This initial process of jamming the human mind with all sorts of garbage is what we Sociologists refer to as *primary socialization*. It is largely unconscious. I do not, once again, mean 'unconscious' in the clinical sense. Here it describes the same mental climate as the mind completely under the sway of the Natural Machine. It is defenseless, and hence *all absorbing*.

From the moment a child is born they are assaulted with meaning. Clean out of the womb a cap is placed on its head — blue or pink — symbolizing this or that gender role that will govern its life[47]. This child is born into a *situation* that immediately begins to shape its perception. There is the

---

[47] For an interesting investigation into what happens to those infants who do *not* fit into these binary sexual categories, see Fausto-Sterling (2000). It is an excellent examination of the brutality of the social world, and its refusal to accept deviation from its mandates.

family it is born into, their socioeconomic status, their moral beliefs, their own idiosyncratic backgrounds. There is also the community it will grow up in, with its diversions, schools, peer groups, crime rates, opportunities for the future, etc.

Aside from situational influences, there are society-wide influences as well. These span everything from the basic building blocks of a civilization — language, interactional norms (such as waiting in line, saying 'thank you' etc.) — to widespread cultural norms. For example, in the United States, the latter include narratives such as 'manifest destiny' (if you work hard you will 'make it') and the blind belief in universal 'human rights'. Personally, I find language to be one of the most interesting of these influences. As mentioned previously, language plays a central role in our experience of reality and is infused with social meaning. Language also distorts and abstracts our perception from the given object we are examining[48]. Much like recollecting a memory, the second a word is attached to an object that object is relegated to a *class* of objects. The unique attributes of this object are deemphasized and lost in favor of the common attributes it has with its categorical comrades.

For instance, this 'chair' I am sitting in is simply a chair. And while it may belong to a sub-type of 'chair' (in this case, an 'office' chair), its labeling as a chair emphasizes its function over its idiosyncrasy. This chair may be better or worse than other chairs in its category; it may be more comfy or adjustable, attributes that will vary by evaluator and method of use. But these are all terms of evaluation attached to it because of its membership in the group 'chair'. I do not consider it as a sculpture or as a natural resource. Its meaning in my mind is limited (at least initially) to the meaning attached to it as a member of a larger category.

---

[48] A favorite topic of study for Phenomenologists and Structural Functionalists.

Enough of chairs—the same process occurs with people. Called *Labeling Theory*[49] by Sociologists, groups are formed within a society's population based on a variety of factors, such as phenotype, reproductive organs, or income to name a few. These categories have a variety of meanings and consequences attached to them, governing everything from how group members view themselves, how they are viewed by others, the forms of behavior they are allowed and expected to engage in, and how they should be treated. While variability certainly exists in how this or that group is viewed by one individual versus another, and while individuals have agency to agree or disagree with the social definition of a group, these 'labels' are widespread throughout a society and are commonly referenced by individuals to determine their views and behaviors toward a group.

Such meanings amount to *limiting*. They function to remove an individual's agency in social situations and guide their thoughts and actions in a certain direction. Once again, not all actions will be the same—you can thank variability in Natural Machines and individual experiences for that. But they are likely to follow the same *pattern*, unless an individual consciously decides to do otherwise. This is the first consequence of social influences.

All these processes and objects also function to inject *meaning* into an individual's life. They are *elusions*. This is the second consequence. From childbirth onward, Society is hard at work building screens and hanging curtains in front of your vision. Sociologists say this is accomplished through *Agents of Socialization*. These involve every individual in your life holding some educative role. These are the people who taught you about 'the world', either formally or informally, including your parents, siblings, teachers, peer groups, mentors, etc. Functionally these individuals are of central

---

[49] Becker (1997). Becker's theory specifically applies to deviant behavior, but it can also be applied to other phenomena.

importance for the successful operation of and changes in Society yet as creatures of Nature they do not behave uniformly.

Variability in agents leads to variability in socialization. This is one of the instances where the natural rears its ugly head. The combination of variance in Natural Machines, social and geographical locations, historical eras, and an almost infinite amount of other confounding effects leads, in turn, to variance in your socialization. This is perhaps why numerous political figures place such heavy insistence on the family, education, religion and whatnot. Variability and conflict in these groups of agents causes discord in the consistent operation of their members. This leads to even greater variation in the socialization process.

These groupings of agents of socialization are what we call social *Institutions*. Institutions can be thought of as the organs of society. They are clusters of groups and organizations that perform similar functions. Examples include the Economic institution, the Religious institution, the Governmental institution, the Media institution, etc. Each performs a central function for the well-being of society, and each is often interdependent on others. But there is opportunity for natural discord on this institutional level as well.

Institutions do not always play nice with one another. The most obvious example is the tension between the economic and governmental institutions, where the latter is tasked with regulating the former; at least in theory. Their relationship is confusing — the power dynamic between the two shifts frequently, and the individuals that act within these institutions commonly transition from one to the other. There are a host of other variables that can confound their relationship, such as the interference of other institutions or extra-societal events, such as wars or natural disasters. The important aspect to note is not that their relationship is in chronic conflict (as the aptly named 'Conflict Theorists' often suggest), but that it is *contradictory*; cooperation at one moment, confrontation the next. The reason why should be a popular refrain by now: while institutions themselves are discursive and created by the actions of men, they are derived from *natural processes*. They are the creations of natural beings operating in a natural world; thereby suspect to the unreasonable, contradictory conditions of natural life.

This analysis is only a quick sketch of the world we live in. Before we confront the quality of the Indoctrinated Self directly, it is important to differentiate between the two types of socialization that give it life.

Up to this point, we were dealing primarily with what Sociologists call *primary socialization*. This is the process by which the individual becomes a functional member of society. It is the basic programming indoctrinated into the person so they can perform the rudimentary functions necessary for modern life. As alluded to earlier, these include the basic rules of society ('sharing is caring'; wait in line), common interactional norms (say 'please'; allow others to speak), and the cultural concepts understood by most in a society (reverence for the military; the importance of money and status; the various categories of human organization, etc.). Primary socialization includes a variety of other aspects as well, but it is best thought of as the individual getting the mental rulebook they need to navigate social life.

There is also *secondary socialization*. This is the more specialized form of indoctrination that builds on the meanings and behaviors of primary socialization. By 'secondary socialization' we mean the focused knowledge necessary for an individual to fulfill this or that social function. The most obvious example is work training. A physicist cannot be a physicist if he does not know math for example. Perhaps the easiest way to conceptualize secondary socialization is for every identity an individual has there is a knowledge base that must be socialized into them. When I start a new hobby, have a child, move to a new community — all these new identities require new meanings and behaviors. Secondary socialization therefore is a process that occurs regularly throughout an individual's lifetime.

Thus we see that basic social control is two-tiered. There is the primary indoctrination from birth, where individuals are defenselessly forced to accept a whole slew of meanings, which they can only challenge (if they want to) after years of subservience. The individual has a world with *depth* forced upon them before they open their eyes. Then there is the secondary process of indoctrination that continues throughout the adult life. It 'ties up' the individual's mind; gives them something to think about. It offers them a stream of specialized elusions they can pick and choose from, while also building upon the primary socialization of their youth. Do I want to be a bodybuilder, a golfer, or a fisherman? It does not matter, as long as I *pick something*. These not only provide meanings and peer groups for companionship, but they also situate the individual in society, give them one of many roles, and further integrate them into it. All your hobbies, relationships, occupations, whatever else; all of them bind you more closely to society and support elusions.

That is, for most people. These meanings can be challenged to avoid elusion and view the world more clearly. I am not saying the Absurdist must become a hermit however, living off bark and pine needles in the forest. Disassociating oneself from the social world eliminates an extremely valuable resource for study. Examining the eluded is one of the best ways to not become eluded oneself (if that is desired). In addition, one can never escape the social world anyway. It is in the very words and thoughts you use. It is in your clothes, your haircut. Just like there is no way out of this unreasonable, uncertain universe, there is no way out of social elusions. All you have is *lucidity* to hold them out from you, examine them, and do with them what you may.

In sum, the social world is brutal. It does not tolerate deviation from fabrication. It is based on familiarity and commonality. The more fractured and complex a society becomes, the more variable its meanings and the more difficult it is to maintain. Ideally, society is a beehive where its inhabitants carry out clearly articulated jobs in clearly delineated groups. But this brutal desire for conformity and predictability runs against every single Natural Machine that comprises its population. Coupled with existing in a natural world, society is locked in a game it will never win.

It should come as no surprise that society, being a social creation, is a reflection of the individual man's desires. It suffers from the same ailments. The only difference between the two is scale and orientation: society is a complex of multiple individuals, and while my Natural Machine is obsessed with controlling the natural world beyond it, society is primarily concerned with controlling the natural world *within* it[50].

Overall, the process of indoctrination is conceptually simple, yet in practice remains complex. This should not come as a surprise — this process takes place in the natural world and involves a natural creature. Additionally, society itself appears simple initially, only to become increasingly complex when its composition and behavior is examined. With this analysis as a premise, the next section examines the *quality* of this Indoctrinated Self implanted in our minds.

ii) The Quality of the Indoctrinated Self

At first glance, the Indoctrinated Self is simply a photocopy of society imprinted into our minds. But this conceptualization is far too simplistic. The character of this construct is far more nuanced than simply being a moral system that acts autonomously in our heads. It is not just a stern school teacher slapping our fingers with a ruler. In this section I discuss a few qualities (but not all) of the

---

[50] Society of course has additional concerns. For instance, it takes action to control the natural world beyond its subjects, such as managing forests to reduce fires and creating public health guidelines to reduce the spread of disease.

Indoctrinated Self. Specifically, I analyze the individual's *experience* of being indoctrinated and the *content* of this material.

The Indoctrinated Self is imprinted *progressively* and *continuously*. Throughout childhood, primary socialization increases in scope and intensity. In primary school, the child is trained to sit still and listen, and the teacher is satisfied with a child who is obedient and knows how to read, write, and perform basic mathematics. These years lay the groundwork for participating in society and the labor force[51].

By the time the child is in high school however, the game has changed. The individual is now being socialized to be a 'good member of society' by learning and agreeing with a variety of cultural concepts. This also involves more advanced, obedient behaviors such as participating in complex task groups. The child is also learning more specialized knowledge corresponding with whatever economic sector they are tracked into. For some its metal shop, for others it is accounting[52]. The key aspect is this indoctrination process is *progressive* — present content builds on the previous. An individual cannot learn the nuances of being a civil engineer if they cannot read, nor can they be expected to get to work if they never learned to stand in line at the elevator.

The progressive character of socialization also explains the significant variability across persons concerning the Indoctrinated Self. Earlier I discussed how variability in Agents of Socialization can cause this. But it is not only differences in the *character* of these agents that impacts the Indoctrinated Self. It is also their *timing*. The influence on an Indoctrinated Self will be very different if an individual learns to read when they are in primary school versus retirement. It is the exact sequence of agents and circumstances that lead to

---

[51] Saldana (2013).
[52] For more information on tracking in public schooling, see Barkan (2013) Chapter 11.2 "Sociological Perspectives on Education".

the idiosyncrasies of each Self. If the Indoctrinated Self is continuously modified and reinforced throughout life, then the sequence of alterations and socializations will have a significant impact on the *quality* of that Indoctrinated Self.

This indoctrination process is also *continuous*. Regardless of how hard the individual attempts to remove themselves from society it will not let go of them. Every time a person interacts with another they are being indoctrinated. Every time an individual interacts with a social object they are being indoctrinated. Every time an individual speaks or thinks a thought, they are being indoctrinated. Our entire capacity for consciousness and experiencing the world is mediated through the Indoctrinated Self. Without it, we are creatures of the forest.

A few examples are in order. Interaction with another individual reinforces a number of different socializations. How the interaction is managed, what is said, how it is said; all of these events reinforce or challenge social norms. If they challenge them, they can either: a) change the individual's perception of the norm in question (thereby fulfilling the natural function of complexity and variation), or b) reinforce that norm in their mind (outrage is an excellent way to socialize individuals into what *not* to be). The same goes for social objects. These are the materials of our modern existence. They include anything from the tangible (magazines, coats, cars, computers) to the intangible (ideas, activities, and meanings). The primary difference between interacting with social objects and individuals is the former generally do not talk back. But the interpretive process is the same. By interacting with them, we either reinforce our socialization or challenge it, in which case we are simply socialized into something else. The key finding is the process happens *regardless* of the content.

Even language and thought do not escape this process. As discussed ad nauseum, language is a social construct that abstracts perception from the natural world. The very words we use are infused with meaning that in turn impact our Indoctrinated Self. For instance, certain identities command certain forms of language; intellectuals are supposed to speak succinctly and intelligently, while gang members are supposed to incorporate a whole litany of slang. Every group has esoteric parlance. But it is not just what form of language is used, it is what that language *does* to the Indoctrinated Self that is interesting. The individual's breadth of vocabulary shapes the nuances they are capable of experiencing. Correspondingly, the meanings embedded in this language reflect not only the character of objects being described, but also the speaker themselves. For example, if you only know ten words, then your experience of reality is going to be rather limited. The more limited your vocabulary, the less variation your Indoctrinated Self can manage. The need to organize experience in a limited set of categories necessarily requires further abstraction and 'smoothing over' of the complexities and contradictions of what is being described. The result is a man with a more limited universe, where objects and processes are simpler, and the individual's experience is less robust.

Thoughts operate in an even simpler way. The thoughts you recall, whether they are memories or ideas, always contain some moral element. They are always desirable or undesirable, good or bad. Attached to each evaluation is a rubric of reasons why such a thought is described in such a way. These reasons are indoctrinated, and engaging in this evaluation either reinforces them or changes them. The type and reasons for this reinforcement or change are socialized into the individual and then spread by them during interaction with others[53].

---

[53] It is important to reinforce that this analysis, at this specific moment, is not taking the Natural Machine into account. The Natural Machine operates according to its own logic, and can also evaluate thoughts, actions, and objects, although it will still use socially constructed categories to do so.

I already spent more time on the progressive and continuous qualities of indoctrination than necessary. We must not ignore examining the *content* of this Indoctrinated Self. What is it? This has already been alluded to: it is not simply society in your mind. Nor is it a disorderly bundle of moral mandates and proscriptions for action. Perhaps the easiest way to describe it is through its counterpart — the Natural Machine.

The Indoctrinated Self is like a Natural Machine that serves a different master. While the Natural Machine propagates natural chaos (by challenging the natural world it is a part of), the Indoctrinated Self serves order. Or perhaps this is better described as *intending* to create *stability*. The supposition that societal action is always conducive to order is a problematic one. Social institutions often clash, the behavior of one society toward another can induce a war, and a society can allow behavior that increases the likelihood of retribution from the natural world (such as disasters). Society seeks to serve itself at the expense of its members, organizations, and even institutions. It is organized to ensure its own continuity. But such self-seeking puts it in contention with the natural world.

Additionally, the Indoctrinated Self's content comes from outside itself. While it could be argued that the *capacity* for having an Indoctrinated Self is innate (it is hard to see how humans could have this feature if it was not[54]), the *content* certainly is not. This is the entire reason why we have so many different human cultures. *Variations in the natural lead to variations in the social*, where climate, geography, and resource availability (among other things) led to significant differences in the evolution of cultures through time. Perhaps the ultimate variation is simply the differential availability and arrangement of specific people within a society at a specific

---

[54] This is not to suggest that animals do not have some version of an Indoctrinated Self either. Some have a rudimentary sense of self-awareness, and many have social structures (Bekoff, 2002). For example, a pack of wolves or an ant colony.

time. If one society happened to have an Einstein, Franklin, and Edison in its ranks contemporaneously and granted them specific opportunities for intellectual cultivation, the history of that society and the world could be significantly different. Differences in the natural base of societies lead to differences in the cultural content of those societies, which in turn lead to differences in the materials used for indoctrination.

But what is that? Once again I hear an outcry! "This Chaos versus Stability argument is a dualism! It is a false dichotomy!" etc., etc. There is no dichotomy here. As I showed throughout this text, while the social may be separate from the natural, it is still the outgrowth of the natural, and thereby still has its characteristics (unreasonableness, contradictoriness, etc.). Additionally, the social world is nested within the natural world and consequently is beholden to its processes and effects. *Society is simply the collective nostalgia of mankind*; the overall will of humanity to fix, explain, and control nature. Even though intentions may differ between the two, they are still ontologically connected and related behaviorally and environmentally. Nature is to society as a mother is to a child; similar yet different.

In sum, indoctrination is constant, and the *content* of indoctrination is highly variable. The important take away from this section is society desires so badly for the Indoctrinated Self to be uniform across its members. This would greatly reduce conflict between groups in society and its organizations and institutions. But human wishes never come true in the natural world. Due to the variability in that world, the process of indoctrination is qualitatively different from person to person. The level of this difference can be significant, and there are arguments to be made that as modernity progresses this difference only grows[55]. But it is

---

[55] Factionalism in American culture is popular topic at the moment. The internet and the rise of ideologically motivated news outlets are creating a situation where the 'facts' that individuals use to shape their worldviews are partisan propaganda that is growing increasingly varied.

also important to not overstate these differences — people still go to work, they still have families, and nearly every single person in the United States has not committed an act of terrorism. Social control may indeed be faltering, but it is still here to stay.

iii) The Process of the Indoctrinated Self

This section focuses on the process and the function of the Indoctrinated Self. At times, comparisons may be made to the Natural Machine, but a true discussion of their interaction and interdependency is yet to come. First, we examine how the Indoctrinated Self operates in the mind, then we discuss how that operation is experienced.

The previous section established that indoctrination is constant. As I hinted throughout this chapter, the Indoctrinated Self is essentially an internalized social control mechanism. It is a kill switch, meant to completely subjugate the Natural Machine. It is also a massive failure. Examples abound that illustrate its shortcomings on a daily basis. People act compulsively, people 'say things they wish they didn't', people hurt others they are not supposed to.

Perhaps the most illustrative example of this failure is the *frequency* of deviance in society. If the Indoctrinated Self and its goal are taken seriously, if we examine its aim to completely control the individual, then we are all criminals in its eyes. Each and every one of us commits deviance on a daily basis; we speed, we cheat, we mislead. Every single occurrence of this situational deviance, regardless of quality or magnitude, is another shred of evidence that illustrates the failure of the Indoctrinated Self. Even if we look at deviance more formally and stick to the cannon of laws, it is still widespread[56]. It is a system incapable of controlling everyone, from schoolboys to the elderly.

---

[56] For example, in 2016 there were over nine million crimes reported to law enforcement in the United States. This figure does not account for unreported crimes (Federal Bureau of Investigation, 2017).

Now the challenge to this proposition says I am catastrophizing — "things aren't that bad". Initially I agree, things are indeed not that bad; perhaps they are *worse*. With the growing plurality of meanings and categories in contemporary society, Indoctrinated Selves are now even more varied and manifold. Consequently, the meanings they seek to enforce in individuals are also different. This serves the interesting function of making moral relativism increasingly visible to the masses, and it also has an extremely negative impact on society. While there is still an 'official' morality codified in laws and mandates, its enforcement and most importantly its *indoctrination* suffer greatly. After all, society must rely on its agents for socializing the masses, yet when these agents hold moralities in contradiction to it, society breeds its own murderers. It may either evolve or die, but the process remains the same.

This analysis paints a gloomy picture. But as is characteristic of natural processes, the Indoctrinated Self is contradictory, even in its *impacts*. Its consistency in failure is matched by its consistency in success. As discussed in the previous chapter, the Natural Machine is constantly moving. Steering consciousness this way or that, demanding this or that behavior, the impression emerges that it operates independently and beyond our control. Even though it often fails, it is very powerful indeed.

But the Natural Machine is not free. While it was first in our minds, the Indoctrinated Self was right behind. From the moment of birth the individual is flooded with meaning, and this meaning does not allow the Natural Machine to run wild.

Can I fail in communicating the importance of not evaluating the Indoctrinated Self solely on the basis of efficacy? While social control is perhaps its primary function (this is something we can never know since society is not conscious; we cannot query it), I would characterize its *most important* function as providing meaning in the individual's life. The Natural Machine provides little meaning. What it does provide is urges – the will to power, the desire for confirmation, the dream of controlling the world. It is the Natural Machine that gives rise to the absurd feeling in man and maintains it. But it is the Indoctrinated Self that provides *elusion*. It seeks to occlude the basic relationship between man and the world, and seeks to infuse man's experience and give it depth.

Often, the Indoctrinated Self is presented as the enemy of the Absurdist. We spend great amounts of time tearing away its veil and striving to maintain our lucidity. But let me make a bold assertion – *we cannot live without it.*

Who we are is almost entirely based on social constructs[57]. Put simply, we *need* meaning to tell us who we are. What separates us from the animals of the forest is our meaning structures. We as a species possess the ability to describe the natural world in a far more detailed and extensive way than all other forms of life. We also use these meanings to describe and reflect upon ourselves. Our *consciousness itself* is only possible through these meanings. If how we think, how we perceive are entirely mediated by these social constructs, then we are nothing without them. If we abandon them, we turn ourselves over entirely to the Natural Machine. We are governed solely by stimulus-response, occupied solely with maintaining our lives. We are essentially lobotomized; we are the squirrels in the forest; hungry, cold, afraid.

But these meanings do not satisfy. They are contradictory; necessary for our lives yet unable to fulfill them. Society offers us so many and we surround ourselves with scores of them. But the sheer quantity of these meanings foreshadows their shortcomings. Cursed with our perception of the human condition we cannot avoid, we still try to forget

---

[57] This assertion has significant consequences for our discussion of the 'soul' in Chapter 8.

the absurd. But we cannot forget it; it is the price we pay for consciousness. All of us know the absurd exists on some level; we at least *feel* it. That is why so many run from it, even killing and dying to get away from it.

As Camus states — "what is called a reason for living is also an excellent reason for dying"[58]. Meanings take on such importance in society that individuals are willing to die for them. They are far more willing to die for *something* than nothing. Through sacrifice, the individual reinforces their belief in whatever meaning. Knowing this beforehand, this knowledge is exceptionally powerful for infusing lives with meaning before the definitive act. Martyrdom, while constantly cognizant with death, is an excellent way to escape the meaninglessness of it.

This condition reaches its height in the warrior. Here is an individual willing to risk the loss of all meaning to gain some. In the kill-or-be-killed world, the warrior finds powerful motivation for behavior and extensive reasoning for survival. In the latter, their survival is not only for themselves, but also their cause (acts of sacrifice notwithstanding). Meaning in this case is contradictory yet extremely profound; urging the individual to put themselves in highly fatal situations, while also urging them to survive. Meaning in this instance drives them toward death, and notions of survival aside, is more important than living.

In sum, the meanings provided by the Indoctrinated Self tell us who we are and obscure the curse of our human condition. We are nothing without them. This finding holds significant consequences for the Absurdist. We see the condition and curse of man far more clearly than most. But we also see the consequences this entails. It is hard to resist the urge to destroy when one masters this philosophy. Like the Marxist, the Absurdist wants to tear it all down, revealing to all the lie they live. But the situation is different in this

---

58 See *The Myth* page 4.

book. Here, we understand that social meaning is not a lie; it is a *necessity*, and we do not exist without it.

The question becomes *what is our task*? Camus said we should stay in the desert of lucidity and not allow ourselves to become eluded. This allows us to clearly see the futility of our actions, which we should perform however in happiness. I must admit this conclusion to *The Myth* does not satisfy me. Perhaps that is why Camus wrote *The Rebel* later; an effort clearly oriented toward infusing meaning into the absurd man's life. The real question is *are meaning and the absurd perspective contradictory? Does meaning always conceal the human condition?*

Once again, meaning — regardless of content — is a process existing in the natural world. Therefore, it is contradictory. At one time in one form, it may serve elusion. At a different time and form, however, it can serve lucidity. It is meaning's utility for lucidity that must be explored in greater depth.

Initially this assertion is unclear. "How can a process that blinds us elucidate us as well?" This question is the equivalent of asking how can water quench our thirst yet also drown us? It is all a matter of situation and quality. The processes of meaning creation, distribution, indoctrination, and performance are so manifold and dynamic in contemporary society that it should not surprise anyone that they can produce amazingly discordant effects. The goal of the Absurdist is to find or create the best situations to encounter and produce the best meanings for evaluating the absurd condition. I am aware this creates a value system; even possibly a *morality*. Well, I would not go that far…but it does require differentiation and evaluation. Without such our goals are unattainable.

Meaning has multiple uses for the Absurdist. Perhaps the two most important are meanings that *focus* the mind on the absurd, and meanings that help *analyze* the absurd.

The most difficult thing the free thinker can do is that initial capturing of the absurd sensibility. Even though all humans feel it with varying frequency, very few *ponder* it at any meaningful length. Humans cannot avoid a conscious evaluation of the absurd — the closer proximity to death, the more this thought pushes its way to the forefront. But to dwell on it and pick it apart in all its complexity we need the help of the Indoctrinated Self.

How does the Indoctrinated Self draw our mind toward the absurd? There are a variety of ways. But first it is important to mention the Natural Machine has little interest in this enterprise. Demanding to be the king of all, it hates examples of its weakness. While the interaction between the Natural Machine and Indoctrinated Self is a conversation for later chapters, we will indulge a little cheating here. To pull the consciousness out of the Natural Machine's desire to look away, the Indoctrinated Self must rely on some rather significant tools.

Perhaps the most powerful is Nature itself. Death is unavoidable, and the monotonous certainty of the event, ever the more likely as each day elapses, pushes this to our consciousness without impetus. It is a calendar game. The unstoppable march of time portends it, as do all the aches and pains in the body. But this is a raw awareness; it is not contemplative. Often, man becomes aware of the certainty of death every once in a while and the absurdity of his existence slaps him in the face. Then he turns away. The awareness of the absurd brought on by Nature has little staying power; something stronger is required.

There are few other tools to do the job aside from our raw awareness of time. Another powerful tool, one with more longitudinal impact, is also a symptom of Nature. Mediating the constant change and dynamism of Nature, Society develops a variety of events that *destroy meaning*. "But I thought Society and the Indoctrinated Self function to *maintain* meaning! That is what you said!" howls the critic. Not so.

Remember, society is a natural product operating in a natural world, and is thereby subject to its forces and characteristics, just not to the same *magnitude*. Society *must* change as time elapses, it simply does so at a slower pace. This change requires alteration or destruction of old meanings to make room for the new.

First a macro level example. Take social movements. Understanding their operation requires understanding the process of change in society. Through processes in institutions such as the economy and science, social objects are created that fundamentally alter the daily operation of society. Telephones, the internet, economic depressions and globalization are just a few examples of these objects. The activities that fueled the processes responsible for creating these objects are done with human hands, driven by Nature and the Natural Machine. But these changes are not without their consequences. They cause alterations and rifts in society that modify how people behave and the meanings they use. These social objects are the "political opportunities"[59] so many social movements rely on for their generation. For example, the rapid rise of capitalism led to Marxism, while the internet spawned online identity politics. These movements can be thought of as the mechanism required for society to cope with change. They create new meanings while challenging and sometimes destroying old ones. They are the growing pains of a healthy society, helping it cope with its structural changes.

Now the micro level. The important consideration here is Society cannot stop Nature. On the level of individual experience, it cannot halt time nor can it stop aging and death. It cannot bring back those meanings the person loved that are now replaced by social changes. The mind is drawn to the inevitability of death and the loss of a meaning system that

---

[59] See McAdam (1999).

structured their personal reality. The absurd condition of their existence rears its ugly head.

They scream out for help; is society impotent? Not necessarily. Even though Society cannot stop Nature, it can infuse these unavoidable changes with meaning. Doing so acts as a healing salve on the mind, and often orients a person's cognition away from the absurd. It is a wipe of the nose and warm hug from the nanny.

For example, instead of thinking about losses and the absurd, a person is encouraged to think about what is *next*. This is reflective of Camus' idea of "hope", where the social pushes man to *look forward to something*, even though this pushing forward of life also pushes forward to death. All that is required is a shift in scope. For example, when confronted with the end of life, an individual's mind is encouraged to take pride in its posterity (children, social impact, charitable works and the like), but it is also directed to focus only on *today*, or at most *tomorrow*. This is a theme you sometimes see in support groups. Even when hope is all but lost, Society still pushes hope, just on a shorter term. And when all else fails there is still that safety net of religion and its ideas of the afterlife. The latter will be discussed further in Chapter 8.

I know I sound confusing. The whole point of this miniature analysis was to demonstrate how social meanings can *induce* an awareness of the absurd, yet I just discussed how they *mask* it. As should come as no surprise by now, this social process is contradictory — it does both. With the evasive aspect of meaning spoken for, we can now consider its elucidating properties available to the individual.

The transition from social meaning to social meaning always contains an element of 'down-time', that tenuous period when one elusion falls away and another has yet to replace it. It is during this time that the social can turn the human mind toward the absurd. These 'social events', or periods of transition between meanings encompasses a wide range of phenomena. These can be both 'positive' and 'negative' in the moral sense, and can include shifts between elusions of various magnitudes. Two examples are necessary to fully illustrate these points.

An example of a shorter term, less salient social event is the death of a pet. There are a slew of factors that can generate variations in this experience (how much you loved the pet; how sudden the death occurred, etc.), but in this instance we will stick with a dog you loved who was in decline for some time. The 'innocence' of the animal makes this experience more poignant — they do not understand what is happening to them, and by all moral evaluations the do not 'deserve' this; they did nothing 'wrong' during their lives. When the pet dies, there is an overwhelming sense of sadness and loss, of emptiness in your life that pet used to occupy. There are the walks that will no longer happen, the toys and treats that are no longer given. This loss induces a fundamental shift in the structure of the owner's daily life. It is this feeling of loss, this feeling of *emptiness* that brings about the opportunity to view the absurd.

Specifically, Society demands we take time to show *grief*. This time is a forced period of reflection on the characters and events of the loss. We are told to *deliberately* avoid bringing new meaning into this segment of our lives — we do not run out and get a new dog. This *period of mourning*, while certainly fulfilling other social functions (such as reinforcing the 'value of life'), is a socially structured opportunity where the individual has lost significant meaning and is provided with a 'hold over' meaning before their 'life goes on' and they acquire a new pet (or do not). This 'hold over' meaning is when the absurdity of death is called into the owner's mind, along with the lack of human actions capable of controlling the actions of Nature.

On a different note, these social events can also be 'positive' and capable of changing the entire direction of an individual's life. An especially salient example in American society is going to college. This process marks a definitive shift between childhood and (pseudo) adulthood, and marks the transition into a more independent phase of life. This transition is usually evaluated positively by the individual and society as a whole.

These two phases of life are often split by summer vacation. This transition lasts months and calls into question many significant meanings in the child's life. Specifically, it can be grievous—weeks are spent in preparation of losing frequent contact with friends and family who were an integral part of their life. There is often significant trepidation as well due to the lack of college experience, changes in geography, and need to create new peer groups. Interestingly, even though this transition is framed positively by Society, it often exacts significant negative affect.

Thus Society creates an opportunity for the mind to turn toward the absurd. Due to their relative immaturity, most of these individuals enact a fairly basic reflection on this condition and are often more concerned about constructing new meaning systems and peer groups in the near-future. In this situation, hope of the future is extremely salient. The loss—however profound—will soon be supplanted by a future full of dazzling distractions (Wednesday night benders, frat parties, etc.). Perhaps to shelter these young minds, when Society decimates one meaning system (high school life and its attendant associations and elusions) it holds out the hope of another far more entertaining system (college life). Unless the individual takes this transition particularly hard, the absurd is often not directly confronted in most instances, but it is certainly felt over those summer months.

The primary function of elusions are to mask our perception of the absurd. Yet when they *fail* to do this they provide the opportunity to perceive the absurd.

That is enough on how Society and the Indoctrinated Self can precipitate consciousness of the absurd. There are volumes of other transitions an individual takes throughout life capable of bringing our natural condition to the forefront.

It is important to focus on perhaps the more important question in this analysis: how do meanings help us understand the absurd? Specifically, how do they help us understand what we do not understand?

The underlying assumption in this analysis is *not all social meanings are elusions*. Is this assumption valid? Or is all thought a distraction from the absurd?

Thought does not distract from the absurd when it is analyzing it. A principle characteristic of the natural world is its *unreasonableness* and the inability of our categories to completely account for it. Note the word "completely". Neither Camus nor myself assert the natural world is completely irrational; that would violate the contradictory character of Nature since it would be setting something constant—Nature would be constantly irrational. By virtue of this unreasonableness alone and the limited applicability of our concepts to the natural world, our meanings *do* have utility for analysis. They explain it...just not very well.

Everything amounts to confusion. But that is alright. Perhaps the best way to determine the utility of meaning for examining the absurd is to make this analysis a matter of method. What tools do meanings bring to the table for understanding the absurd? This is the ultimate testament of their utility, and in this light they are extremely useful.

While there is no shortage of meanings that *distract* the individual from the absurd (first and foremost, religion), there are a precious few that show us its colors. Absurdism itself, along with Existentialism, Irrationalism, Phenomenology, Social Constructionism and various other systems of thought—even Marxism to a limited extent—tear away at that veil of elusion. At least initially. As mentioned here and throughout *The Myth*, all these philosophies reveal the curse of meaninglessness in the human condition, only then to paint over it with the most splendid of colors (except Absurdism). This unpleasant characteristic aside, these are all meanings that, albeit temporarily, reveal the lack of depth in our universe.

The next logical question is the *degree* to which these meanings are useful. That is an easy one — *they are not.* The Existentialists and others reveal the apparent meaninglessness of the universe only to then graft a new meaning over it; religion for Kierkegaard, communism for Sartre. While knowledge is an interesting learning exercise, it is only a point on the philosophical map, not their destination. The method that deliberately *refuses* to elude — Absurdism — is left to *describe* the relationship between man and Nature, for anything beyond this leaves the plane of evidence for belief[60]. You either get brief knowledge covered by art or limited knowledge covered by nothing.

Are you satisfied knowing only that you exist and this world exists, and that this world is largely unreasonable and contradictory? Wait — I hear more critics: "Then everything in this book is lies! If that is all we can know then how can you make all these statements about Society, Nature, and Man?". Point well taken. If the reader looks beyond the rhetoric and inductive reasoning, they will find this book produces no more real knowledge than they already knew. All I did here was sketch out the walls that confine you more clearly. Everything written to this point can be (and often has been) contradicted. It is still just *You* (who you do not really understand) and that *World* there (that you really do not understand). All I did is drive home the point.

Perhaps now is a good time to take a matinee from our analysis and pick up a case study. I think one will suffice in this instance. I choose the Leftist movement in 19th century Europe to illustrate this analysis of the Indoctrinated Self.

---

[60] This is a reference to Camus' notion of "level". See page 36 of *The Myth*.

iv) An Example of the Indoctrinated Self: Leftism in 19th Century Europe

This topic could be a book in its own right. Here I limit myself to the more consequential characteristics of society and the Indoctrinated Self for our analysis. Specifically, I examine the plurality of Indoctrinated Selves, their socialization into social movement membership, and their contradictory nature in this movement.

At its root, Marxism is the perfect expression of splintering meaning in western society. It was born out of an unignorably severe social condition — the extreme deprivation and brutality of the early capitalist system. This was a time when humans lived and died at work simply because they were always there. Children's hands were being ripped off in coal mines, and the value of every man was in how much they could work, how quickly they could work, and how expendable they were. In other words, there were a lot of Natural Machines around that were being brutally suppressed by Society and their own Indoctrinated Selves that demanded conformity. It was only a matter of time until something happened.

And that something was Socialism, and all its wondrous variants. From the get-go, Socialism was manifold. Fournierism, Nihilism, Marxism, Bakuninism, Kropotkinism, Proudhonism, this 'ism' that 'ism'…lots of 'isms'. While such an occurrence certainly speaks to the immense social opportunity for change during this time[61], it is also an excellent illustration of the extensive variation in Indoctrinated Selves.

The condition of the 'proletariat' was universally dreadful. Sure, there was variation in severity and in quality of life, but the basic level of existence for a vast majority of the population was simply unsustainable. The level of international foment that occurred within a relatively short

---

[61] What Sociologists call "political opportunity", see McAdam (1999).

amount of time (historically speaking) is a testament to this. But the interesting thing is if conditions in Europe at the time were so terrible across the board, and if this was all mostly due to the same social process (rapid industrialization), then why were there so many different currents in this single movement?

This variation in the movement can be explained with the Indoctrinated Self. It also, contradictorily, created even more variation among Indoctrinated Selves. The fascinating aspect about this historical situation is that even when conditions were so uniform across multiple countries, there was still a significant amount of variation in minds[62]. Different theories appealed to different minds (let alone those who chose Liberalism instead)...*why*?

Because every Indoctrinated Self, no matter how uniform Society attempts to make its conditions, is still a natural product of the natural world. Variations in this world from place to place and time to time, coupled with variation in agents of socialization and differences in individual natural machines leads to a universe of completely unique Indoctrinated Selves. And when confronted with social conditions that so desperately needed to be addressed for their survival, different minds went different ways.

This universalism of suffering and variation in rectification strategies is so emblematic of the natural world. But some forms of Socialism eclipsed others. Why did this happen? One explanation is the varied efficacy of socialization.

Some men are more gifted wordsmiths than others. Karl Marx — albeit not the most accessible of writers — explained the current conditions in such a thorough and persuasive way that an army of men who probably did not

---

[62] This is not to de-emphasize the difference between sectors of the capitalist economy or differences between capitalism's operation in different countries. There was still plenty of variation to go around. I would assert, however, there was *less* social variation during this time period than in others.

completely understand him was born. Other traditions (such as Social Anarchism) achieved their own successes as well. As known by social movement scholars for decades[63], effectively socializing individuals into your movement is as important as securing resources for its success. With slogans like "Property is Theft"[64] and the utilization of frames[65] about justice and sharing, many of these groups were able to use highly salient meanings in western society against that society. Those capable of making these connections appeared to be more successful[66].

Across the board, alterations to the mass of Indoctrinated Selves was relatively easy. Multiple traditions in social movement theory agree the time was ripe for revolution[67], and institutions such as the *First International* and universities provided resources and manpower to spread the gospel. The sheer volume of tracts and texts produced during this time was simply staggering. The vastness of materials distributed, the significant number of revolutionaries crisscrossing the continent, and the ideological variability in the Socialist movement itself greatly increased the likelihood of successful indoctrination. Due to the significant variation in Natural Machines and Indoctrinated Selves in society, the more angles used to present an idea the greater the likelihood of indoctrination in total. Even those that were not entirely

---

[63] Which includes your author.

[64] Proudhon (2008).

[65] Frames refer to "schemata of interpretation" an individual uses to understand the world about them. See Erving Goffman's *Frame Analysis* (1974: 21) for a more detailed explanation.

[66] This is by no means an empirical statement, but respected research in the field does concur (McAdam 1999). Other movements at the time—such as the Flagellants in Russia—were more oriented toward religious atonement than justice. Their movements suffered accordingly.

[67] For instance, the Political Process Model would certainly agree that working conditions and the tenuous nature of nascent capitalism constituted a "political opportunity" (McAdam, 1999). Relative Deprivation Theory would argue the reality of industrial labor was not in line with workers' expectations. For a review of the latter, see Gurney and Tierney (1982).

convinced (such as liberals in Russia) were still closer to leftist radicalism on the ideological spectrum than in decades past.

While recruitment and indoctrination may benefit from such variability, this phenomenon also reflected the contradictory nature of the Socialist movement. As discussed above, this ideological fracturing certainly limited the movement's prospects for success, and reflects the natural and contradictory attributes in all social movements. But perhaps the greatest example of contradiction in this movement was its *praxis*; a fancy academic term for how theory is put into action.

When it came to the consistency of means and ends, the Socialist movement was far from consistent. In many instances the goals of the movement were vague and ill-defined, and even when they were defined there was little direction for their institution. At one end of the spectrum were the Russian Nihilists, who simply wanted to destroy the current order with little consideration about what should replace it[68]. On the opposite end were the Bolsheviks, who rose to prominence in the early twentieth century with a clearer conceptualization of what soviets were, what their goals were, and how they were to operate.

In addition, the tactics for achieving this or that socialist utopia were almost always violent. Assassination attempts were commonplace, and purges were often implied or openly advocated[69]. With this in mind, the fundamental contradiction of the *process* of the Socialist movement begins to take shape. On one hand, Socialism of more or less all stripes proclaimed its desire to institute a new world order where workers were in control and egalitarianism reigned free. The quality of life was certain to be exceptional. On the other hand, the methods for bringing this utopia about were far from democratic. Those in power should be forcefully removed (usually slain), and all their supporters exiled to

---

[68] For an excellent literary example inspired by historical events examine Pyotr Stepanovich, a main character in Dostoevsky's *Demons* (1995).
[69] For example, see Kautsky (1919).

somewhere or executed. The Russians and French illustrated the brutality of this orientation exceptionally. Of course, as Max Weber tells us[70], once social organizations are created they rarely die. In fact, they tend to propagate themselves. It is only a movement of ignoramuses (and educated ones at that[71]) who could think social structures used for killing and destroying would suddenly become warm and embracing when it was time to build the new society. Russia and North Korea are excellent examples of this failure to adapt.

<u>v) In Conclusion</u>

In sum, Society and the Indoctrinated Self appear to enforce *consistency* on the world and the individual respectively. But both are outgrowths of natural processes and both also exist in the natural world. Therefore, man's crowning achievement — his attempt to hold the world and the self as constant and to completely manipulate them — often achieves the opposite. Variance and contradiction creep into institutions and minds, and simple social processes and structures become complex. Things change, and Society and the Indoctrinated Self cannot stop it.

Now we understand the terms of the game. There are two opponents who are not always opponents. The field of play is constantly shifting; one day a tennis court, the next day a boxing arena. Both teams swap players and sometimes score against themselves. The scoring system itself remains unclear. All contributes to confusion and complexity.

In the next chapter we examine how this game is played.

---

[70] 1958.
[71] Marx for instance had a PhD and Pyotr Kropotkin was a Russian aristocrat.

VII) (Dis)synthesis: The Relationship Between the Natural Machine and the Indoctrinated Self

This chapter examines the complex dynamic between the Natural Machine and the Indoctrinated Self. It also includes a discussion of the relationship between the natural world and society. The directions this chapter could take are manifold and the topics nearly infinite. For the sake of simplicity, I discuss only two topics: the *adversarial* relationship between the Natural Machine and the Indoctrinated Self, and their *cooperative* relationship.

i) The Natural Machine versus the Indoctrinated Self

The individual's mind is a battleground. Consciously and unconsciously aspects of himself, natural and indoctrinated, push and shove each other trying to control consciousness. At least this is one way of thinking about it. While far more complex in reality, in this section we take the adversarial relationship in the mind as constant.

Take a moment to envision the mind of a man torn apart by these warring attributes. It is chaos. At one moment, he is a model citizen, waiting patiently in line for a train ticket. At the next moment, he is shoving fellow passengers out of the way and grabs the ticketing clerk through the bars of his window. His ticket must be purchased now — in fact he does not even want to purchase it, he wants it *given* to him. The picture emerges of man as a child at best, schizophrenic at worst.

Now then, why does this not happen with regularity? Why are suited and booted businessmen not throwing old ladies out of cabs and punching their way to the front of lines? I offer an assertion — because *the Indoctrinated Self is more powerful than the Natural Machine*. "Wait" you say, "doesn't this fly in the face of an underlying argument in this book? That Society and the Indoctrinated Self are natural products in a natural world, and thereby beholden to its characteristics? Didn't you say the Indoctrinated Self was a massive failure?" Well, yes and no.

As stated before, the manifest function of the Indoctrinated Self is to dominate the Natural Machine. Its strength and nuances are the masterpiece of humanity; our greatest creation. Yet it varies from individual to individual due to the confounding effects of Nature. This refresher aside, it is time to explore the validity of the proposition that the social aspect of man is more powerful than the natural.

Everything in contemporary society asserts the opposite. In a world where the physical sciences reign supreme and elites do not want their systems of power challenged, it should come as no surprise that so many aspects of the individual are chalked up to the innate qualities of the natural. Genes make you who you are; your environment may mess around with them a bit, but their fundamental characteristics do not change. But I assert that this social meaning proclaiming the dominance of physical science is, in fact, a *social meaning*, propagated by a society that seeks stability and desires innate natural aspects that cannot change. Specifically, these meanings are supported by individuals in society who have a vested interest in their adoption by the masses (governmental elites, economic tyrants, scientists, medical doctors, etc.).

To be contrarian, my assertion in the opposite — Society and Indoctrinated Self call the shots — is substantiated simply by these very assertions of the supremacy of Nature[72]. Nature trends toward variance in worldviews, and hostilities between biological and social explanations of human behavior are just

---

[72] I am aware this argument borders on the tautological, and I do not care. Tautological critiques are the home of scientists who lack valid criticisms of an idea, so they rest their egos on the assertion that arguments are flawed since the solution implies the problem. It is intellectual petulance.

one social meaning fighting it out with a competing social meaning. The fact remains that all explanations are still social meanings — previously it was God who called the shots, not Nature and biology. This macro social analysis translates directly into the individual mind.

The Indoctrinated Self wins over the Natural Machine simply by our capacity to reflect on the Natural Machine. We can hold it apart from us, examine it, and put it back on its shelf. The Natural Machine does not make the Indoctrinated Self an object of study in such a way; it is more concerned with *action*. "But does that even matter?" I hear you say. "So what if it can look at it; it can't *do* anything to it". According to this logic, we are all just window shoppers peering through the glass at products we can never afford. No one can smash the display.

Except, of course, the Indoctrinated Self *can* impact the Natural Machine. But the analysis now shifts to the level of *magnitude*. This is the central aspect to consider when evaluating the 'power' of the Indoctrinated Self. A solution was already hinted at — the Indoctrinated Self may be able to *shape* the Natural Machine, but the natural process still runs the show. The Indoctrinated Self relies on natural physical structures to exist, and is nested in a world that operates according to natural logic. The Natural Machine is the engine that drives the human process forward, while the Indoctrinated Self steers it slowly and to a limited effect.

This would make sense if the natural world made sense. This proposition articulates a *constant*; the interaction between the Indoctrinated Self and the Natural Machine is permanently structured in such a way that it can never change. But Nature does not allow constants, it demands variance. Therefore, if our logic holds, there *must* be instances where the Indoctrinated Self dominates the Natural Machine.

It just so happens there are. *Sacrificial altruism* comes to mind. In this instance, the Indoctrinated Self hijacks the Natural Machine to annihilate itself. Specifically, the social meanings vested in the Indoctrinated Self are so powerful that they are capable of overriding the primary concern of the Natural Machine—confirmation. The Natural Machine cannot confirm itself if it is dead, plain and simple. It would be one thing if the Indoctrinated Self simply "disabled" the Natural Machine and carried out its work without it, but in this instance it actively *uses* the Natural Machine to achieve its goal. An example is necessary to illustrate this idea fully.

I recall a news story when I was a child. A person was trapped under a crashed helicopter, and a (rather large) bystander lifted the helicopter enough, single handedly, so that the trapped person could get out[73]. In this instance, the moral mandate in the Indoctrinated Self—specifically the demand that we *empathize* with others[74]—overrides any sense of self-preservation demanded by the Natural Machine. On top of that, this process of empathizing is so effective, that when the individual sees this trapped person and imagines their state, they experience the same hormonal and metabolic reaction that person would. In this instance the bystander had such a strong and significant physical reaction to this psychological process that his body literally gave him the strength to lift the helicopter. Thus a metabolic process that the Natural Machine usually reserves for itself to aid *its own* survival is transferred to another individual it never met. This single moral mandate socialized into the Indoctrinated Self, not even relying on other mandates such as friendship or familial ties, was enough for such an amazing action.

The Indoctrinated Self does not appear debilitated after all. In certain circumstances, it is capable of overwhelming the consciousness and forcing its will on the Natural Machine. But is this the trend or the exception? I can produce a variety

---

[73] There are multiple examples of feats like this; try a *Google* search.

[74] In Sociology we call this taking the "attitude of the other" (Mead, 1934: 134). It allows individuals to put themselves in another's shoes so they can align their behavior with social expectations, leading to smoother interactions. See Mead (1934) for an extensive examination of this topic.

of other examples (religious asceticism, military sacrifice, etc.), but these instances are remarkable precisely due to their rarity. Society makes a grand show of such acts as 'heroism'; there are parades for them. Their moral prestige unsurpassable, they are held as the exception to the rule. And what is the rule? It is what I see walking down the street. Downcast eyes, quick steps filled with intention, individual goals that demand they be achieved. These people are stuck in the automata. Extraordinary acts of empathy are extraordinary because they run counter to the vast average of 'normal' existence. They are surprising only because they break with the norm of (un)consciousness.

Thus ends my consideration of the power of the Indoctrinated Self over the universe of the human mind. Its might culminates in the occasional spark of dominance which quickly fades. It finds itself more often relegated to butler of the Natural Machine — setting its tasks for the day, cleaning up after it, trying to influence it, but in the end going along with whatever it wants. It shapes the Natural Machine in *form*, rarely in *content*.

Now, time for the opposite argument — the Natural Machine calls the shots in the mind. There is this psychological vestigial organ in modern man called *instinct* and *reflex*. These behaviors occur without permission from our Indoctrinated Selves; they are Nature taking the reins out of Society's hands. But is this the best argument we can proffer? I give you unbreakable circular arguments when I discuss the Natural Machine's adversary, but now, even with all that was stated as evidence of this creature's strength in previous chapters, now all I can come up with is *reflex*? Allow me to try my hand again.

Calling it a butler is too generous — the Indoctrinated Self is nothing but a *slave* of the Natural Machine. Sure, slaves may rebel and seek the death of their masters. Occasionally they are even successful at this. But in the aftermath, their 'free' societies they are so fond of constructing just make them subservient all over again. Before, it was subservience to a king. Now, it is subservience to a legislature. The masters are greater in quantity, the masters are even elected, but they are still masters. Such is the same with the Indoctrinated Self. It its slavish subservience, it lashes out, seeking to overthrow those despotic and disgusting natural aspects of the mind. It fails, over and over again, but it still tries.

Through these repetitive attempts, it may even succeed in changing the Natural Machine to some extent. A social product, the Indoctrinated Self is always changing. The Natural Machine, being a product of Nature, is not immune from this disease either[75]. This is often expressed socially as the individual learning to 'control themselves'. *Patience* is perhaps the most profound manifestation of this process.

When born, the human is in their most primitive state. More like the slug than their parents, the infant seeks immediate satiation of natural requirements to confirm the existence of their Natural Machine. Its cognitive capacities are completely limited to stimulus-response logic. It demands that its needs be met now. This is a process that continues throughout childhood. Yet slowly and surely, as the child is reared and enters school, their socialization gradually eats away at the *immediacy* of the Natural Machine. The Indoctrinated Self places more and more powerful restraints on its sudden lashing out. While the Natural Machine certainly does not consent to this, it soon finds that restraint is not without its advantages. Rewards are given to the child for demonstrating constraint, specifically for delaying the confirmation of the Natural Machine. The child begins to learn and the Indoctrinated Self begins to support the idea that *waiting* can often lead to greater rewards than what is

---

[75] It should go without saying, but there is a preponderance of evidence illustrating how the social world shapes the natural world. From deforesting a landscape to increasing the risk of cancer due to pollution, the actions of society often have the consequence of changing its habitat. This can either be deliberate or not, but change still occurs.

initially desired. Furthermore, this repression of the Natural Machine by the individual spares them from having it repressed by agents of socialization, who often apply more severe consequences than the negative affect the Indoctrinated Self does. The Indoctrinated Self demands cognitive and affective concessions, while people on the other hand often demand material consequences as well[76].

But even during the process of *patience* that underlying impulse and drive of human behavior is always the same — *confirmation* of the Natural Machine. The only reason why it commits to patience is that a momentary denial of confirmation holds the prospect of even *greater* confirmation in the future. But this is a rather bold statement; in fact, the previous discussion of altruism calls it into doubt, along with the credo that no process is constant in the natural world.

"But Sociobiologists tell me this is the case! The individual always strives to maximize themselves." That is, until they do not. Here is an opportune moment to discuss *suicide*, and the consequences it holds for the hegemony of the Natural Machine.

As previously stated, Camus masterfully addresses this issue in *The Myth*. Here I will not give it such an extensive treatment, but I will view it from a slightly different perspective. Suicide is turning the Natural Machine away from the world. It is giving up. It is a process, therefore, that is saturated with profound meaning.

Suicide is perhaps the most meaningful act an individual can do in their lifetime. It can also be done for a variety of reasons. But most importantly, the consequence is always the same — the meanings that lead to the fatal act destroy the very organism that embraced them. It is the triumph of meaning over the natural. In the language of this

---

[76] This pattern does not hold out over the entirety of life, of course. The Indoctrinated Self does make material demands on the Natural Machine in adulthood, such as saving for retirement.

book, it is the only way the Indoctrinated Self can defeat the Natural Machine.

But how does this occur? Well I cannot completely say because I am not suicidal. But we can use our methodology to perhaps shed some light on this fatal process.

Quite simply, the Indoctrinated Self has to provide a compelling enough *reason* to not only hoodwink and hijack the Natural Machine for its ends, but also to convince itself that its own elimination is desirable. This is a herculean effort of logic. Perhaps the most convincing way to examine this question is to look at situations where the Intellectual Self is capable of convincing itself that it is *not*, actually, destroying itself.

Enter the pantheon of religions and their doctrines of eternal life. Religions know the afterlife is a powerful notion; it can be exceptionally useful to rulers for inducing mass sacrifice in a populace. But the sheer power of this notion is not without its dangers. "If I am going to be teleported to a celestial paradise at the end of my life, why should I bother dealing with all the pain and discomfort of living? Why don't I just kill myself and cut to the chase?" This is indeed an enticing idea if you believe this doctrine. Religious officials are clearly aware of this, and many include in their cannons a prohibition against exactly such a drastic act[77]. Suicide amounts to cheating; it is having desert before dinner. While martyrdom is certainly messier, it achieves the same effect while also promoting whatever religion, and is therefore supported more by clergy. The fact remains that doctrines of eternal life without balances to keep individuals alive have the potential to be quite homicidal.

Magnitude of impact is another consideration when examining how a person cons themselves into death. It is possible for an individual to believe that the impact of their

---

[77] For example, Christianity (Cholbi, 2017) and Hinduism (Subramuniyaswami, 1992).

act will grant them a sort of 'practical immortality' in the annals of culture. Falling on the sword for something 'greater than themselves' can be thoroughly motivating, as it was for Yukio Mashima[78]. While the individual's physical form may be destroyed, their *will* continues through the act's impact on society. This is certainly a significant gamble, as the individual has no control over how their act will be interpreted, nor can they know this ahead of time[79]. In this case, immortality of the self is traded for immortality of *impact*, and the Natural Machine can be made to feel confirmed. Society is always changing however, and social impacts blow like leaves in the wind; once they were here, now they are gone[80]. This complicates the effort of the Indoctrinated Self to induce these acts in the individual, often requiring a reference to some sort of movement or historical process that the individual is a part of[81]. While this dilutes the individual's impact (now he is simply the representative of a movement greater than himself), it increases the likelihood that the act will be evaluated positively and remembered longer by comrades in arms and society in general.

Enough of these musings on those rare instances when the Indoctrinated Self subdues the Natural Machine. These contrarian points can be taken too far. We must not overemphasize the exception to the rule. Yes, the chaotic, unreasonable, contradictory characteristics demand that no rule be universal, that no constant remain constant. The only constant is change. So it comes as no surprise that we can find exceptions to the hegemony of the Natural Machine in the

---

[78] While there is debate regarding the true intention of Mishima's *seppuku*, the argument still stands. See Nathan (2000).

[79] Camus provides a rather humorous footnote on this conundrum in *The Myth*, page 7.

[80] What was prominent in the past is often not what is prominent today. Consider how often you think about other 'Social Saints', such as Andrew Carnegie or Christopher Reeve.

[81] This is a common theme in revolutionary and reactionary movements, and spans groups from the Continental Army in the American Revolution to ISIS suicide bombers.

human mind. But that does not alter the *trend* — the Natural Machine is driving a significant majority of man's everyday action.

Additionally, just because a Natural Machine is in the 'flow' of enacting a meaning that does not mean it ceases its chaotic shifting. As discussed previously, the Natural Machine is firing off memories and thoughts almost constantly in the mind. And no matter how hard an Indoctrinated Self may persevere to limit the content of these firings, the random nature of the Natural Machine wins out after a time. Thoughts that have nothing to do with a task enter our minds.

Let us return to the street, to the throng of people wading down the sidewalk, going from social situation to social situation to fulfill this or that need for confirmation. They go to work or home to their families, to breakfast or the pharmacy. These distractions they flock to serve a confirming purpose. And this brings us to the most important topic in this analysis.

ii) The Natural Machine and the Indoctrinated Self

The Natural Machine needs elusions, and it relies on the Indoctrinated Self to provide them. It is a mistake to define the relationship between the Natural Machine and the Indoctrinated Self as purely antagonistic. Until now this is mostly what I did. But here I say it is quite likely their relationship is more *cooperative* a majority of the time. This does not mean they cleanly coordinate their actions to achieve a common goal. What it does mean is they will not stand directly in each other's path for the *survival of the whole.*

You see, while the Natural Machine is likely to behave in ways that maintain itself[82], I fear our previous analysis

---

[82] But not always, as that would be a constant. Drug use and poor diet are examples of how the Natural Machine is often very shortsighted when it comes to seeking confirmation. Our discussion of patience aside, the Natural Machine tends to be more of a short-term player.

gives the impression the Indoctrinated Self is far more lax when it comes to self-preservation. This is not precisely true. Yes, the Indoctrinated Self is the product of Society, which prioritizes the survival of itself and its institutions than any single blood cell coursing through its organizations. But a vast majority of its efforts are also coordinated toward individual preservation. Most of the goals and hopes it feeds us tend to promote pro-social behavior that integrates the individual into the social fabric and elongates our lives[83]. If it were the contrary and the Indoctrinated Self drove individuals to isolation and self-destruction, it would be the equivalent of societal suicide, one blood cell at a time.

Both the Indoctrinated Self and the Natural Machine appear to strive toward maintaining life. That is why they need each other. Specifically, that is why the Natural Machine needs the *elusions* the Indoctrinated Self provides.

The problem with humanity is we are too smart for our own good. Our natural development outpaced our natural capacity. Cursed with the ability to understand our common situation, we are marooned by nature with little ability to *handle it*. I am thoroughly convinced that if a man does as Camus says and remains constantly lucid to their absurd condition and the complete inadequacy of their understanding and action—I am convinced they will annihilate themselves. What soul could take the constant reinforcement of its own insignificance without seeking to escape it, either by the knife or the theater? No natural creature can exist in a constant state, and any attempt to do so will lead to flight, one way or another.

This brings us back to our discussion of meaning in the previous chapter. I stated that meaning was imperative for us to understand who we are; it is what separates us from beasts.

---

[83] This most commonly manifests in examples of what we 'should do'. Society tells all of us we 'should' exercise, we 'should' eat well, we 'should' create bonds with others and help them as they help us. These mandates also include an affective push as well, making us feel upset if we do not follow them.

Here, I go even further. Meaning not only shows you who you are, *it is who you are*. The Natural Machine, by definition, is devoid of any stable content. Constantly oscillating from this endeavor to that, it is a *process* of action seeking confirmation. This confirmation can take a variety of forms, and the Natural Machine is fine with that. It is the intended *result* that drives it.

The Indoctrinated Self on the other hand is both a process *and* content. It is the process of consistent socialization and curtailment of the Natural Machine, but to achieve this it must utilize meanings. These meanings in turn are stored in our natural structures and referenced continually to achieve these goals. But these are more than tools of its craft—meanings take on more than a utilitarian character. They literally become *who you are*. The Natural Machine provides no real morality or role in this world, its only morality is self-satiation. It does not tell you who you are, it just tells you *what it wants*. The Indoctrinated Self though, it both paints and *is* the most glorious and beautiful picture known to man.

The Indoctrinated Self is our artistic triumph. Confronted with a natural world that we are aware of yet do not understand, it dresses our selves in a protective barrier of meaning. Suddenly, actions that were merely instrumental for survival now become shrouded in significance. Me myself, who I am, is also clothed in meaning. Sitting in a chair, doing nothing, I still have meaning divorced from action. This meaning can be general—"I am a good person"; "I am intelligent"—or more specific—"I am Johnathan from Freeport and I like to paint fruit". It provides us with a worldview and a path—"I am Christian"—and with an intention for our lives—"I exist to (fill in the blank)". This process is inescapable; no matter how much the Absurdist may try to tear away these meanings he wears, *he is still an Absurdist* with his defined task. *These have meaning for him*; they cannot be eluded.

This is where we circle back to elusion. This chapter is supposed to be about the interaction of the Natural Machine and the Indoctrinated Self, and it is important to explore the consequences of these meanings for the former. We already skimmed the surface of this analysis; meanings are tools for the Indoctrinated Self to control the Natural Machine. A key principle of religion, this meaning system can be extremely effective at denying the Natural Machine certain courses of action. It seeks, quite simply, to limit the most animalistic inclinations of this beast.

But meaning fulfills other functions as well. The most important is it prevents the Natural Machine from destroying itself. Not only by placing prohibitions on action; but specifically by *enabling* the Natural Machine to enact its character. This is a central aspect of this analysis and requires sufficient clarification.

From what I can tell during this analysis, the Natural Machine is prone to chaos. Its method for seeking confirmation is unreasonableness. It throws our consciousness here or there, and searches every nick and cranny for something to occupy itself. The issue is, when left alone without its companion the Indoctrinated Self, the Natural Machine is severely limited. A creature of the present, it soon becomes frustrated with the options available to it. Why do you think humans were initially nomadic? Sure we had to move to secure food and primitive resources, but then why did we continue to move after the rise of agriculture? Why do we explore? Our Natural Machines drive us to. Sitting on a rock in the forest, my consciousness is initially engaged. I hear birds and look for them, I examine the bark of the trees and the moss on the ground. Such diversions hold my interest for a good five minutes. Then, my mind is off somewhere else. I feel two impulses — I must either move to find other things to experience, or I dive inside my mind to create my own mental experiences. My natural aspect is not satisfied for long; it demands *action*.

This is where meaning serves such a pivotal role for the Natural Machine. Why else is humanity driven to create? Why do we construct societies and cultures with such complexity? Because we do. We are *driven* to. In its constant search for satiation and confirmation, our natural selves demand new material. It is a constant painter who is always running out of oils and canvas. This is where *elusions* become so necessary for our *survival*.

The Indoctrinated Self feeds the beast. It has to, or the beast will devour itself[84]. Thus it seeks out elusion after elusion, meaning after meaning that both direct our gaze away from the shallowness of human existence and, quite simply, give it something to do. As a natural process, we can be sure of two things when it comes to the Natural Machine: a) it will be chaotic and unreasonable, and b) it will be constant and unstoppable.

This process of feeding our Natural Machines is especially important in the modern world. So many prohibitions on the Natural Machine are required for so many people to function in so little space. The simple fact is we cannot allow it to run as free as it did in the past. The demands of urbanization and capitalism require such. This is perhaps why *cities* have the most spectacular elusions in a society. This is also perhaps why the city is sought out by so many.

Here the senses can be overwhelmed with meaning and pursuits. Here, in the constant crush of people, one loses themselves in the collective pursuit of confirmation. It is a carnival of ideas and distractions, where the tools for self-realization are plentiful and so is the content to fill the self. Other authors decry the metropolis, saying that it leads to anomie[85]. Yes, the brutal complexity and variance in meaning certainly does challenge the more homogeneous culture we

---

[84] I proffer this assertion as a leading reason for suicide.
[85] See Simmel (1969).

had prior to globalization, which certainly can cause strain in the individual and a feeling of disorientation when it comes to worldviews and perceptions of self. Sure, the metropolis also demands that individuals make an *immediate* impression, for the constant flow of urbanites glosses over idiosyncrasies and sabotages opportunities to create relationships with new people. But one has to ask if these disadvantages are not acceptable in comparison to the metropolis' advantages. Sure, there is a challenge in making one's impact felt which can entail negative consequences for the Natural Machine, but this is a struggle it experiences everywhere. What the city provides, however, is far more *opportunities* for confirmation, and this characteristic is what makes it invaluable in modernity. In an interconnected world where individuals feel increasingly anonymous, the city offers them a nearly infinite amount of opportunities to try their hand at new elusions for achieving self-confirmation.

Not everyone moves to the city of course. Others prefer the rural districts, where confirmation can be found by simply enduring the natural world. The options for elusion are certainly curtailed, but they are not necessarily less profound. It is here that we encounter the age-old juxtaposition of *quality* versus *quantity*. The metropolis floods our minds with an amazing quantity of experiences. There is so much variety that one feels like a chameleon capable of making themselves whatever they want to be. Such a social environment appeals to some more than others. At the other end of the spectrum is a focus on the *quality* of experience. When one is confronted with many identities, meanings, and elusions, they can all create the impression of being *expendable* — "if this doesn't work out I'll just give something else a try". This expendability can in turn lead the individual to become not as attached to these meanings — these meanings simply do not have as much meaning to them. This is not as significant a problem for the rural man[86]. His options significantly curtailed, he turns his mind from the greatest *quantity* of experience to the greatest *quality*.

This is where we find individuals who appear to never change. The archetype of the parochial farmer who lives on his land for decades and rises every morning to tend crops is a persistent one. We put it on tubs of butter. But if you look more closely at these individuals you will find an experience with more *depth* than first thought. There is plenty here for the Natural Machine to feed on. By working so close to Nature these individuals experience its unreasonable and contradictory character much more profoundly. In response, their elusions must be all the more powerful to fend off consciousness of the absurd.

Take the cow farmer. I had the opportunity to observe these individuals in my youth. Here is an occupational elusion that confronts the individual with natural processes constantly. His livestock is marginally controllable. They can be driven in general directions as long as they remain in their pens. They are large animals capable of wounding or killing him. They demand their food enthusiastically and fight one another for it. They are relatively insubordinate and untrainable in these conditions[87]. In short, they are raw nature confined by social objects.

But the socially constructed parameters placed on their existence are routinely violated. Some cows attack others. Some cows break out of their pens. They constantly piss and defecate all over their enclosure, requiring the never-ending task of mucking up. Ringworm spreads like smallpox. When

---

[86] Of course, with the internet the capacity of elusion is increased in rural districts. Individuals can achieve a whole variety of identities and encounter so many meanings virtually without ever leaving their homes. The utility of this phenomenon for the Natural Machine is manifest in the success of the video game industry. With one click of the mouse I am a wizard, the next an assassin. I am allowed a shadow life where my Natural Machine can run free without any of the consequences.

[87] Yes, I have seen cows capable of being led on halters and performing a variety of tricks. But in the demands of the agricultural setting, there is little time, interest, or lifespan for this training to be accomplished.

leading them across a parking lot, some of them refuse to touch their hoofs on the white lines. When one looks close enough, there is a never-ending litany of occurrences where the natural revolts against the social constraints place on it.

Robust elusions are especially important in these situations. It is here that the individual is constantly confronted with the unreasonableness of Nature. How do they respond? They define themselves *against it*. Nature is something to be overcome; it *must* be overcome for their survival. Thus they cultivate and develop one of the most amazingly important elusions for human existence — *mastery*. They do not occupy their Natural Machine with a never-ending flow of elusions; they pick one and derive all the consequences from it. It becomes a game of skill, not speed.

Mastery in this scenario is belief in one's capacity to control the natural, or at very worst to *endure* it. The entire persona of the 'rural man' is built around the *practical control* of nature. These individuals are expected to have an extensive knowledge of how to fix things, how to make it from point A to point B, of 'what will work and what won't' in whatever practical situation. Meaning is found in their potential to cause *impact* in the natural world, which must not be confused as having an *understanding* of it. There is a reason why individuals in rural districts are far more religious — they likely understand *less* about the conditions of the natural world and human existence. Their lifestyle often *avoids contemplation*, and instead focuses on action and impact. It is the Natural Machine's dreamland[88].

Such is a reason why many rural people commonly define themselves in contrast to the urbanite. In the city, there is *too much* contemplation. The variety of meanings challenge central meanings in the Indoctrinated Self, and here is an

---

[88] Must I remind the reader that this is not a value judgement? There is no assertion here that the urban man is 'better' than the rural. Absurdism is a method, not a moral rubric. My only interest is thorough analysis, regardless of consequences.

excellent example of a place where myths of mastery go to die. There is no livestock to coral or trees to fall; the opportunities to control raw nature are extremely limited. If one wishes to compensate and instead attempt to control others in the city, aggression from the urbanite is the least of their problems. Confronted with this, the rural man characterizes urban life as relatively useless — they don't 'know' anything, they have no 'practical' skills — and then describes himself as living a 'real' life he has mastery over. The urbanite applies a variation in turn (rural people are 'hicks' and culturally depraved, for instance). Class and racial stereotypes abound, and in the end they reinforce the meanings they want to believe anyway.

Not all (or even many) people who live in rural areas are farmers of course. There are software developers and insurance brokers who make their homes in less-developed country. But the process is the same. Often, their hobbies and pastimes are centered around confronting and challenging nature (fishing, hunting, hiking, etc.). Even simply *existing* in these areas provides significant meaning. In the advanced North, 'sticking it out' through the winter is an achievement in and of itself. Such an existence maximizes contrast in comparison to the 'flatlander' or whatever derogatory euphemism for 'city folk' they come up with.

In short, the rural man escapes the absurd condition by *embracing* the natural. They eliminate a necessary precondition for maintaining the absurd position — *revolt*[89]. By embracing the difficulty of existence and defining themselves as *masters* over it, they provide their Natural Machine with a feast of meaning. While the variety of meaning is nowhere near as extensive as those offered to the urbanite, these rural meanings appear far more powerful.

There are other ways the Indoctrinated Self and Natural Machine coordinate efforts. I will limit myself to one more topic.

---

[89] See pages 53-55 in *The Myth*.

While the Natural Machine needs the Indoctrinated Self to feed it, the Indoctrinated Self also needs the Natural Machine to produce this meaning in the first place. Specifically, the Natural Machine *breathes* life into the social meanings that are a part of and created by the Indoctrinated Self. The relationship is *cyclical*, and is broken into four parts: Necessity, Creation, Consumption, and Excretion.

One could say the only reason any social meaning exists in the first place is because of the Natural Machine. Remember: in our primitive yet overdeveloped capacities, the Natural Machine has a greater appetite. Our evolved consciousness is capable of examining the world and ourselves in far greater detail than other animals, yet these natural aspects are still more powerful than our social ones. We are, essentially, children holding machineguns; we have *capacities* far beyond our *maturity*, and knowledge of this ailment does nothing to relieve it. Consequently, our Natural Machines are extremely active. They demand the elimination of the absurd by controlling the natural world and require a greater variety of situations to provide confirmation.

The natural world in its naked state cannot provide what our Natural Machines demand. It refuses to capitulate to our desires, causing us to turn away and seek confirmation elsewhere. Additionally, the natural world is inadequate at providing a sufficient *variety* of experience for our Natural Machines as well, simply because everything natural resists our manipulation. Faced with a world I cannot understand that will not provide me with sufficient opportunities to confirm myself, I am forced to look elsewhere to find self-verification. This is why meaning, a social construct, is so necessary for our natural aspects. We desperately *need* it.

We just examined at length the next element of this relationship. Once meaning is necessitated it is *created* by the Indoctrinated Selves that comprise society. It is the human miracle and necessary ointment to relieve the demands of our Natural Selves. The next step is the *consumption* of these meanings. This is often the moment when our consciousness is lost. This is when we plunge ourselves into the *flow*[90] of the task, when we pass over into our most natural manifestations. The Indoctrinated Self sets the stage and the rules. In a day, it provides a variety of meanings that can be adopted and acted upon. We simply choose what we *feel like* doing. This is the Natural Machine taking the initiative. While the meanings we adopt and enact[91] throughout the day are in the most pedantic sense the product of pure choice, the Indoctrinated Self clearly values some more than others, and Society places a variety of consequences and prohibitions on them. Except in those with weak Indoctrinated Selves and/or extremely strong Natural Machines, the choices tend to be prosocial.

So here we are, enveloped in whichever process our Natural Machines choose. We labor away at this or that, and in so doing expend energy and tire ourselves out. This is good; a fatigued beast is far more capable of being controlled than a raging one. Eventually somewhere in this process our Natural faculties will tire to an extent where the Natural Machine wishes to end participation. This is furthered by its chaotic desire to experience something different. After enough time, no one wants to stay in the first act of *Hamlet*. We are all eager for the story to progress.

So our Natural Machine has all its little projects. Many of these are *longitudinal* — they cannot be completed all in one go. This also benefits the Indoctrinated Self and Society, for it is far easier to control and predict the Natural Machine's behavior if they can manage to keep it engaged in some meaning. Whenever the Natural Machine fatigues it can be shifted to a new, less strenuous task. Or if a Natural Machine grows bored with a meaning, it can be shifted to a new, more entertaining project. This *shifting* is initiated by both natural and social forces — I can get frustrated and want to do

---

[90] See Csíkszentmihályi (1975).
[91] Importantly, not all meanings need be enacted immediately upon their adoption, but all appear to have consequences for behavior.

something else, or my shift at the factory can end. The important thing is regardless of the impetus, every meaning process ends. This means there must be sufficient meanings to transition to, and they must have sufficient variation to accommodate all statuses of the Natural Machine.

The consequences of not having a well-stocked Indoctrinated Self can be severe. This is an issue we addressed here and there in this text. Too long of a transition between meaning systems maroons the individual in their existence. They suddenly feel the emptiness of time, the shallowness of the human experience. They are confronted with a stale world they do not understand, and the feeling of the absurd begins to grow. Camus states in *The Myth* how *boredom* leads to the growth of the absurd in a man. The Indoctrinated Self *needs* to avoid this.

This situation introduces the last stage of this codependent process. It is what I call *excretion*. All things that eat shit. The Natural Machine is no different. Eventually during its consumption of meaning systems, the Natural Machine 'gobbles them up'. The process comes to an end, or the meanings are past their sell by date. With a creature that is constantly on the move, meaning systems that are not linked to a specific, completable task are expendable. It is only a matter of time until the Natural Machine tires of them and seeks something else. This falls under the *excretion* concept as well.

Defined concisely, *excretion* is that transitory time between meaning systems. There is a whole universe of these systems, where some exist on the macro plan and grant meaning in a general sense, and others are specific to certain tasks. Macro meanings often have a variety of behaviors attached to them that may overlap with other macro meaning systems[92]. Their micro level counterparts are often nested

---

[92] Here I am essentially describing 'social identities'. See Stryker and Burke (2000) for a good example of how these operate and interrelate.

within these macro meanings and apply to a single task within their repertoire. For example, I can define myself as a mechanic a thereby do a certain type of work in certain types of places. Within this meaning system of 'mechanic', there are multiple tasks that correspond to that identity with their own rules and procedures (for instance, changing tires, tuning engines, etc.).

Importantly, the excretion process still remains even when the experience of meaning systems changes. When I finish a task at work and become bored I do not call into question my entire career[93]. My Natural Machine simply feels strain since it has nothing to consume in that moment. It shuffles through the library of memories and meanings built by the Indoctrinated Self to find something else to do. It may choose to act or play a 'memory movie'. Excretion is that searching that exists in the hole of time between meanings and tasks.

I provided examples of this process in a previous chapter[94]. It is enough to say that excretion is an incredibly *dangerous* time, especially for the eluded man. The more the person lives in the veils of illusion, the more desperately they cling to them. If it is a macro level meaning system that was recently excreted then the situation is even more dire. Society and the Indoctrinated Self strive with all their might to fill these holes in time, and deploy all the grandeur and splendor of modernity to achieve this. But the clock is ticking. If it is the excretion of a *micro* level meaning then the individual may simply act out of hand or daydream. But when it is a *macro* level meaning the individual may result to desperate measures. These include initiating significant life shifts (moving or taking a new job) in the *best* of circumstances. Often, this 'dead time' can lead one toward either self-elimination (depression and/or suicide), deviance, or other

---

[93] Yet if it happens with great frequency it may spur a shift in this relatively stable meaning system.
[94] See Chapter 6.

anti-social inclinations. Regardless of what level the meaning is there are consequences, but their seriousness usually increases in significance the more macro they become[95].

Living is hard, especially in modernity. While the entertainments are nearly endless, the *depth* of experience for the modern man is certainly less than the parochial one. Confronting nature directly provides the rural man an advantage in this regard, but there are fewer and fewer rural men left. As urbanization and development increase so do the opportunities for elusion, but at the price of a shallower experience.

The cyclical, codependent relationship between the Natural Machine and the Indoctrinated Self reveals the seriousness of our collective situation. If this cycle is broken, trouble almost immediately sets in. If this 'break' is prolonged, the consequences can be extremely serious. Neither the Natural Machine or the Indoctrinated Self want this to happen, but the natural world cares little about desires or intent.

iii) Conclusion

What did we derive from our examination of the relationship between the Indoctrinated Self and the Natural Machine? It is important to clearly state the principle results of this investigation:

a) The relationship between the Indoctrinated Self and the Natural Machine is *complex*. Since both are outgrowths of Nature (the former indirectly and the latter directly), they exhibit its characteristics to different extents. The key characteristic is the *contradictory* nature of this relationship. At one moment, the Natural Machine is exercising its dominance over the Indoctrinated Self. At the next (rarer) moment, the relationship is reversed. Often, they both work in a loose state

---

[95] There are *meso* level meanings as well. Existing in-between macro and micro level meanings, these constructs contain qualities of both. These meanings are not examined here; see Bourdieu (1984) for a more detailed explanation.

of cooperation, with the Indoctrinated Self taking the role of the responsible parent, and the Natural Machine acting as the petulant child.

b) The relationship between the Indoctrinated Self and the Natural Machine is *cyclical.* It is also *codependent.* This codependency begins with necessity, then transitions to creation, consumption, and the excretion of meaning. After excretion, necessity demands that creation begins again. This interactive process does not cease until death or incapacitation.

c) The relationship between the Indoctrinated Self and the Natural Machine is *necessary.* Evolved to our current state, we are cursed with a consciousness that cannot help but contemplate the absurd. Self-destruction is likely if we are left alone to this endeavor. For our Natural Machine to survive, it needs the elusions and meanings from Society in the form of the Indoctrinated Self. Once meaning excretion is achieved, the Natural Machine howls with hunger and must be fed. Sustenance is required not only for the Natural Machine's survival. Without our physical form the Indoctrinated Self does not exist either, and without an army of Indoctrinated Selves Society also does not exist. The continuation of human existence depends on this process.

Now we have an understanding of each element in the human mind and the world, including how they interrelate. All that remains is to extract all the consequences from these findings.

VIII) Consequences

This analysis holds a variety of consequences capable of impacting nearly all aspects of how we understand ourselves and this world. In this chapter I focus on three — the Soul and Afterlife, Morality and Systems of Belief, and Everyday Life.

i) The Soul and Afterlife

This topic harkens back to the last chapter and our brief discussion of the afterlife and its consequences for suicide. In this section I discuss the validity of the existence of an afterlife knowing what we now know, followed by a similar examination of the existence of the soul.

This is perhaps the most troubling topic for the mainstream reader. The Natural Machine, quite simply, does not want to die. Much of modern society is directed toward distracting the individual from this eventuality[96], and it infuses life with meaning as if to delay its onset. And so we have relationships that matter, jobs that matter, hobbies that matter, and a healthcare system built to extend all this 'mattering'. Perhaps the most significant manifestation of this mattering is the common belief found in nearly all societies on the planet — there is *something* after we die. While there is significant variation in how this 'something' looks, it is often an eternally shining, resplendent, mythical world where the Natural Machine is constantly satiated.

Now we just need to follow our method and examine this construct with the concepts we already developed. We immediately know that the notion of any afterlife is a social construct. It is not purely natural. It is a textbook elusion, for it seeks to hold constant a specific state of being. In nearly all its manifestations, there is no contradiction or lack of clarity in its meaning. It is often spelled out with clear intent as to the

---

[96] But not all, see Chapter 6 section iii) for a discussion of meaning that leads to loss of life.

character and structure of this state of being. This further supports its status as a social construct.

The next consideration is what function it could possibly serve for the common man. This consideration extends our initial thought. It is a *certainty* applied to the most *uncertain* aspect of human experience. None of us know what it is like to die because none of us are dead. Sure, there are examples of individuals being resuscitated and 'coming back to life' as it were, but by their very ability to be resuscitated their experience of death was short and, most importantly, incomplete. Such lack of consciousness is equivalent to sleeping; whatever we bring back with us is primed by the material world, yet not of it.

The sheer magnitude of uncertainty the afterlife attempts to resolve is enormous. It is one of man's most important and difficult projects. The afterlife is not just necessary to ease the strain of unavoidable annihilation on an individual mind. It is also extremely important for maintaining the stability of meaning systems across a whole society. As alluded to previously, without some *post mortem* event, the human mind often begins to dwell on what 'all this is for'. Stripped of a guarantee of permanence, the actions of the individual take on their true character — they are *temporary* and *meaningless*. "If nothing is meant to last, then what is the purpose of doing *anything*?" the idle mind asks. This is why the afterlife and its sister concept *legacy* are so important; they organize the whole suite of an individual's behavior. Without them, justifying this or that action becomes increasingly problematic.

We should continue to broaden this concept beyond its religious overtones. When we include any *post mortem* meaning in this concept, it becomes particularly applicable to the modern sentiment. Atheism is at an all-time high. Many loudly proclaim it, pinning it like a medal on their chests. When I encounter examples of this inclination there is still meaning that is sought. Instead of creating a positive impact on this or that god, the atheist now seeks a positive impact on society, often with *post mortem* intentions. Functionally, such amounts to the same thing as the afterlife, although this endeavor is likely significantly less satisfying due to a lack of metaphysical or spiritual content.

It hardly requires much persuasion to demonstrate that concepts such as the afterlife and posterity are extremely important in most societies. But what are the *consequences* for this concept when subjected to the absurdist methodology?

The simplest explanation is the aforementioned argument: the afterlife is an elusion meant to calm man in the face of his unavoidable death. But this is too easy; it relegates this concept to the common pot of diversions and does not recognize its extraordinary status. Absurd analysis reveals something else: not only is it *necessary*, but the concept of afterlife (religious or secular) is *unavoidable*; it *must be adopted* by every Indoctrinated Self.

This, of course, presupposes that the individual is not suicidal. Since this concept is derived from nature, we will always be able to find contradictions and exceptions to it. Fair enough. But for the man unwilling to feel the cold breath of death, he *needs* some construction of the afterlife to maintain him until that fateful moment. We already examined this necessity previously. But the *unavoidability* of this construction is perhaps the most consequential for our analysis. No matter how hard a man may strive to look at the sun, if he does not protect his eyes with *something*, his retinas will burn out. Even in the most analytical, secular man, the *hope* is unavoidable.

Take Camus for example. The man who proclaimed the moral equivalence of all meaning and the profound lack of any depth to the universe still clings to the hope of posterity. This is illustrated by his *actions* (for why else write books if but to ensure your ideas outlive you) and by his *philosophy*. Regarding the latter, *hope* for the future is attacked as being a principle agent of elusion; focusing on desires for the future keeps many men distracted from the absurd. There is certainly a preponderance of evidence supporting this assertion. But the basic framework of the absurdist methodology leaves room to hope for the future as well.

The entire stance of absurdism is to 'live without appeal', to rely only on what we know. This is an excellent proposition. Yet throughout *The Myth*, there is a mature understanding that a variety of explanations for how the world works *may* indeed be true. We just do not know if they are correct, and as a responsible scientist no assumptions should be made. These 'maybes' that live so strongly in the popular imagination are hopes that everyone — including the Absurdist — certainly want to be true. As Camus states, the existence of an angelic, immortal afterlife would indeed be highly desirable[97], we just do not accept as truth what we do not know.

The consequence of this situation is simple — I do not know an afterlife exists, but I sure hope it does. Perhaps more befitting my inclinations, I do not know if anyone will ever read this, but I sure hope they do, *especially* after I am dead. Hope is not antithetical to Absurdism. It should be noted as unavoidable, yet should not influence our method or behavior. An honest man will admit they have hope. If they do not, they are either lying (most likely) or they will be dead soon.

Turned away from the absurd condition, man is safe from it for the moment. That is until they look too closely at *themselves*. This is where the question of the 'soul' emerges, which is highly consequential for the common man.

Exploring the soul is a favorite endeavor of mystics and theologians. Its existence is taken for granted in many religious traditions. Because who would want to say no? In Christianity for instance, the permanence of the soul is a necessary condition for the afterlife; if the soul is not

---

[97] See page 53 in *The Myth*.

permanent but the afterlife is, then what does it matter? But let us look beyond this superficial longing and give this idea the treatment it deserves.

Following our method and what we know from this analysis, the answer regarding the fate of the soul should be *contradictory*. This leads to my following assertion: the soul exists and is not immortal, but is *recurring*. This assertion is based on Nietzsche's idea of the 'Eternal Recurrence'[98]. In opposition to Christian conceptualizations of time, this notion asserts that time is not linear, but *cyclical*. While the Eternal Recurrence is based on some rather significant assumptions, it has analytical utility for this analysis. Specifically, if time is constantly infinite, and the amount of matter in the universe is set, then it is only a matter of time until all events are once again arranged in the exact same manner as they are right now. This is basic probability theory — if you have a set amount of combinations and an unlimited amount of attempts, it is only a matter of time before any given combination repeats itself.

This logic can be applied to the soul as well. While I am deliberately refraining from discussing the *content* of the soul at the moment, it is assumed when applying this framework to the person that if their lives are again arranged in the exact same way they will have the exact same personality, consciousness, and disposition. Everything that makes them 'who they are' , the content and quality of their minds, should be identical to what it is now. This assertion is problematic however when the assumptions it is based on are examined. As discussed at the beginning of this book, physical science is not free from the absurdist method. Its instruments, premises, and controls are all socially constructed, and reflect the prejudices of their creators. There is no 'objectivity' in this science.

---

[98] See Kaufmann (1974).

Therefore, when I am asked to base my understanding of the soul on these scientific assumptions I quickly feel the need to turn away. If it is not something immediately perceptible to me, that I cannot *experience*, then I am abandoning my method for speculation and art. I do not want to speculate; I want to *know*, and now must return to the drawing board.

Now I pose a different argument. I can avoid all this nuance and intellectual strain by simply asserting that the soul does not exist in the first place. First, I state what is often defined as 'the soul' is simply a rebranding of consciousness. Waylaid without Psychology and Sociology, the ancients did not have the most thorough understanding of the structure of the human mind. The simplest explanations ruled — whatever godhead created the world and everything else also created the soul.

Explanations for why things occur and why we are supposedly eternal are most convenient when they emanate from one source. Eventually, man's growing awareness of the complexity of existence requires a pantheon of gods responsible for this or that, but this is only a minor inconvenience. Stating that the soul simply 'is' because god created you is far less strenuous than any systematic introspection of its ontology.

Thus the ancient understanding of the soul is filled with celestial assumptions that horrify the absurd man. It is easy to disprove such constructions in our modern age even though many do not wish to. These elusions aside, I support my assertion that the soul does not exist with evidence from this study. Specifically, I suggest that the 'soul' as it is called is the combination of the Natural Machine and the Indoctrinated Self. It is, simply, the totality of the mind.

This is an additive argument. At the beginning of this book I went one step further, asking if the soul was an *interaction effect* of the Natural Machine and Indoctrinated Self, where its existence is born from the interaction of these two concepts yet is greater than the sum of their parts. Knowing what we now know at this stage of our analysis, I proceed first by determining if the soul is merely an additive combination of these two processes in the mind. Then, if necessary, we explore the interactive possibility.

From the additive perspective, the soul is a Janus. It takes on the characteristics of both the social and the natural. This assertion has significant consequences for how we understand ourselves. By merging attributes of the two, the soul is schizophrenic in character. It is contradictory and unreasonable, yet desires with all its heart to be consistent and constant. This conceptualization meets the demands of our methodology by proceeding from the findings in this analysis.

In this additive analysis therefore the soul is the Absurd. It is an individual distillation of this broad socio-natural process. The 'essence' of each individual is the tension between what it is and what it wants to be. The *magnitude* of this tension, mixed with the events of an individual's life, are what make him unique. All man 'is' hinges on how the contents of his soul are prepared; we are simply mixtures. These assertions require additional exposition.

The key attribute here is *variability*. When an infant is born tension between aspects of the mind is basically non-existent. As previously discussed, the newborn has more in common with the frog than man; they are the naked embodiment of the Natural Machine. In this state, they have constant desires which demand to be satiated. The infant thus comes into this world as a creature of it, yet concurrently at war with it. The child is completely occupied with challenging the natural world for satiation.

But the Indoctrinated Self takes root rapidly and with it the demand for *consistency*. While the Natural Machine demands to be consistently satiated, this consistency is part of an inconsistent process; what the Natural Machine desires often changes. The Indoctrinated Self on the other hand demands total consistency across the individual, in his thoughts *and* his behaviors. This is where the confrontation in the self emerges — between what his Natural Machine *is*, and what his Indoctrinated Self *wants* him to be, yet chronically fails to achieve. This is the absurd condition *within* the human mind.

Elements of this conclusion were already mentioned throughout this text. But there is a key consequence of this thought that must be stated clearly. *We, ourselves, are living, breathing manifestations of the absurd.* It is structured in our minds and inescapable. We rapidly learn to live with it thanks to Society and its army of elusions to choose from. But it is still *there* and unavoidable. The loosely-structured chaos we see in Nature is *us*, too.

Now we come to the *difference* between the minds of individuals. A critique immediately comes forth: "If all we are is the absurd, then why aren't we all the same? Why is there variation in personality?". There is variation in the minds of individuals because minds are derived from the natural; it is as simple as that. Specifically, we are discussing variation *in* and *between* the Natural Machine and Indoctrinated Self. Previous chapters discussed the variation *within* these constructs at great length. This accounts for part of the variability in individuals. But there is also variability in the *interaction* between these two elements. In each mind, there is that absurd divorce between what our Natural Machines are and what the Indoctrinated Self wants us to be. The magnitude of this divorce also shapes the character of the soul.

Considering the degree of this tension has the prospect of explaining a broad range of human behavior. First, the magnitude of divorce is on a continuum. For the human to be truly human, they cannot be all Natural Machine or all Indoctrinated Self. The first is an unconscious invalid, and the second a computer program. Where you are lies in-between. Similar to continuous variables in statistics, it is possible for this range of variability to be effectively infinite[99]. Therefore, it is possible for every single person on this planet, no matter how many there are, to be *unique*[100]. While Person A may appear to be exactly the same as Person B, it is possible (*if* the absurd is continuous), for them to vary by .000001 on this continuum. It may not be much of a difference, but it is still a difference. Even if there is a limit to the subdivision of this continuum, there is still variability within it, satisfying the natural demands of our method.

But how does this look practically? Well, first it will likely appear *innate* to many individuals. It will often be confused as variation in the Natural Machine itself, not in its relationship to the Indoctrinated Self. This is because both forms of variability express themselves similarly. For example, an individual with a powerful Natural Machine versus another with an unbalanced relationship between their natural and social aspects are both likely to be deviant. In each case, Society's mental leash on the individual is weak, either because the natural is too strong or their socialization is inadequate. While it is certainly likely that these two conditions covary, this is not a requisite. An individual can certainly have a relatively 'inactive' Natural Machine, yet because their socialization is so poor, the absurd in the individual is more oriented toward this natural aspect's confirmation.

This gets to another important consequence of the absurd in the human mind. Depending on the balance between the Natural Machine and the Indoctrinated Self, the soul may either be more inclined toward *confrontation* or *elusion*, respectively. A less restrained Natural Machine will savagely attempt to dominate the natural in whatever situation it finds itself. Such individuals are likely to be at best

---

[99] Continuous variables are capable of being subdivided infinitely.
[100] This is similar to a Phenomenological analysis that could assert all material objects vary from one another, regardless of how strict the categories for grouping them.

manipulative or at worst homicidal. Those on the opposite side of the spectrum (a highly restrained Natural Machine) are potentially more prone to withdrawal from the world. Confronted with situations they feel incapable of effecting, they seek refuge within their minds. Additionally, they are likely to be more susceptible to influence from the Indoctrinated Self, possibly causing them to be overly sensitive to social norms. Examples include a wide variety of human states, from those with social anxieties to those who are social 'dropouts'; those who seek refuge in books and those with various substance dependencies. These individuals spend their entire existence turning *away* from confronting the natural, while those with savage Natural Machines strive to dominate it.

This variability in the absurd is not all that contributes to variability in the soul. While we are discussing a more internal process this does not originate or operate independently from its environment. As discussed previously, our perceptions of the world and the content of the Indoctrinated Self originate externally from the individual. The absurd process in the mind requires *content* to deliberate, and this content also contributes to the variation in souls.

While my assertion of the uniqueness of the absurd divorce appears likely, the idiosyncrasy of individual life experiences and content appears even more so. This analysis is far less strenuous and its obviousness should increase confidence in its veracity. We know from previous analysis and our own experience that no one else has the exact same history as we do, simply because there was never — always — someone else there. No one truly has a *'constant* companion' in their lives. Our unique collections of experiences and memories guarantee idiosyncrasy in our souls. All events change us; we learn, we are hurt, we forget, we recover. The experience of these events, our reactions to them, and the consequences that result all contribute to our uniqueness.

Cognitive relationships and content aside, there are certainly even more confounding effects causing variation across souls. It is not the purpose of this analysis to articulate each one. All that interests me is demonstrating that each soul is *unique*. To do so we needed to understand how these souls worked and what comprised them. Our newfound understanding of them holds significant consequences. By following our method, we assert the soul is: a) the characteristics of the Natural Machine and Indoctrinated Self; b) the absurd process born of the interaction between these two components; and c) the content of the lives we live, and all the consequences we derive from them. Arguments can be made that this or that component should be added to this analysis. Such is fair, and it gives academics something to do. The important result is our method reveals who we are — the content and operation of our soul — and this is based at least partly on the absurd process *within* our minds.

Now time for some rejections. It should go without saying that this analysis rejects any assertion of the immortal character of the soul. With death, the Natural Machine ceases to be, and the absurd process is ended. We also reject the ideas of the afterlife or reincarnation from religious doctrine. While hopes for posterity remain, these hold no consequence for our understanding of the soul; anything left behind after death is not the soul itself, and without its process or content is ceases to be. Lastly, if assumptions of infinite time and finite matter are upheld, this analysis is not in conflict with Nietzsche's 'Eternal Recurrence'. But owing to our rejection of assumptions, we cannot support his concept.

The final task in this analysis of the soul is to determine either its *additive* or *interactive* character. The preceding analysis should make this decision obvious. One of three core aspects of the soul is born only from the interaction of its components. The absurd *process* in the soul cannot be understood by simply adding together the effects of the Natural Machine and Indoctrinated Self, nor is it just a byproduct of the cyclical nature of their interaction[101]. The process of their interaction remains separate from other processes that shape the equilibrium of their relationship. Additionally, the soul is a compendium of memories and consequences from life, balancing its processes with its *content*. In sum, the soul cannot be thought of as simply the summation of the natural and social elements of man. It is a mixture of multiple processes and a lifetime of content.

This is enough discussion on the soul. The findings of this abbreviated analysis are simple. We only have this one life, and who we are is a torrent of activity and material. We are, therefore, natural. Take whatever you will from this.

In the next section, we discuss the consequences of our analysis for meaning, morality and systems of belief.

ii) Meaning, Morality, and Systems of Belief

Perhaps the best way to start this section is to consider the following: What does this analysis tell us about morality and belief that Camus does not?

Camus was relatively circumspect in his examination of these constructs: in the most simplistic of interpretations, they are simply elusions. He proffers that "everything is permitted" to the lucid man, for he lives only with what he knows and morality is relative[102]. While there are other nuances to his analysis, these remain the definitive points. It is not my intention to critique Camus' work; that is what graduate students are for. Instead, I show how my analysis builds on his.

Perhaps the most significant difference between the two is my assertion that *meaning is unavoidable and necessary* for the survival of the individual and Society. It affixes itself to us when we are most vulnerable and it cannot be completely cast off. Without meaning we cannot reflect on what little

---

[101] See Chapter 7.
[102] According to Camus, man only knows he exists and the world exists, but the quality of both mostly escape his understanding. See page 19 of *The Myth*.

understanding we have of this world, nor can we examine the absurd. Sure, a majority of meanings lead to elusion, but not all, and elusion is a necessary element of all individuals since our Natural Machines will not permit us to focus on any one topic (let alone the absurd) for a significant amount of time.

This difference between analyses also extends to morality. Camus frames this as a *choice*. Since "everything is permitted", it is up to the absurd man to choose his own path, as opposed to blindly aligning his actions with the mandates of society. Morality in this book is treated more analytically. When socialized into the Indoctrinated Self, it is not as easy as simply 'deciding' to engage in behavior contrary to a moral code. The Indoctrinated Self will actively work to constrain behavior, usually through negative affect. Additionally, the function of the moral code becomes clear during our analysis, where it is a social attempt to fix meaning in a world that is filled with variance and is constantly changing. By considering the individual as nested within a socio-natural world, the forces that act on him become visible.

Analysis of *belief* on the other hand is commensurate between these works. In both instances, meaning systems are based on presuppositions, not scientific observations. They are what man *wants* the world to be, not what it is, and are thereby ideal examples of elusion. Beliefs are interesting analytically, for they reveal the mindset of the eluded man and reflect what Nature does not fulfill in him, but they are not a course of action for the absurd man.

Therefore, while this analysis has some significant differences yet also some similarities with Camus' analysis, I have yet to fully address its *consequences*. When reflecting on this study as a whole, a theme begins to emerge. I call it *freedom*. This is not the same concept as Camus'; it is actually almost the opposite. Camus argues that hope and nostalgia are the principle culprits of elusion; when man relies on them they infuse him with a whole universe of meanings that distract from the absurd. I assert the contrary. Meanings, when used appropriately, are the fuel for a man who desires to break free from elusion. A conscious soul that *understands* how elusions function can construct his own meaning systems that avoid them.

As a free man, I can create and arrange meanings that lead me toward the absurd, not away from it. I can simply reinterpret all the behaviors and objects in my life as manifestations of the absurd. This dovetails well with Camus. Just because I do the same thing as the eluded man, it should not be mistaken that I do it for the same *reason*[103]. This is why Camus asserts the employment of the absurd man is insignificant, it is more about how he *conducts* himself. This notion of freedom is applied to everyday living in the next section.

Freedom aside, what is the consequence of this analysis for the meanings and moralities I was socialized to fervently believe? What happens to the individual when they become fully aware of the socially constructed nature of these meanings? The answer is simple. They become *responsible*. Just because a man becomes aware that 'everything he believed in' is not completely verified by Nature this does not mean he becomes a psychopath. It simply means he must make a choice. All too often, when people feel this dilemma growing within them they quickly attempt to squelch it before exercising their freedom. If this analysis taught us one thing, it is Nature and Society will never allow us to be free. We are scared to explore these topics because they threaten the comforting certainties we once had. We become nostalgic as Camus says. Doing so amounts to eluding our full human potential.

This eluding is enabled by the contradictory character of nature. There are examples in the world that can confirm essentially any meaning, moral, or belief system a man wishes to be 'true'. Sure, it will not actually be 'true' because contrary

---

[103] For example, see pages 90-91 in *The Myth*.

evidence can also be found, but if the individual is satisfied with *some* validation of their beliefs and is willing to disregard evidence to the contrary then amends can be made. If I want to believe with all my heart that nature is inherently creative, then I can just look at babies and sprouting leaves. If I want to believe that humans are inherently 'good', then I can simply recognize only those acts of kindness I see on a daily basis. Everything is capable of becoming what I want it to be, as long as I am resilient in my desire to see everything that way.

This brings up an interesting (yet unsurprising) contradiction concerning freedom. In its pure form, freedom is liberating. It is the *intentional* exercise of my ability to generate meaning. When combined with an absurd sentiment, it allows me a sharper image of the human condition. On the other hand, most individuals practice a bastardized form of freedom that has more in common with slavery. Here, freedom is *reactionary*, and is not really freedom at all. These are the situations where one feels a twinge of doubt, the possibility of a meaning system ringing hollow, and instead of interrogating that meaning and constructing new meanings, the individual runs away from the challenge and attempts to create new meanings supporting their chosen system. The Indoctrinated Self senses danger, and the individual heeds the negative affect to compulsively create. Responsibility is abandoned, and the architect becomes the slave of the meaning system they serve.

The consequences of this analysis for meaning, morality, and belief could fill another book. At this point, we step outside abstract conversation and observe how our findings apply to everyday life.

iii) Everyday Life

I start this section by returning to our discussion of *freedom*. Specifically, I am interested in how the absurd freedom to create and organize meaning is reflected in the everyday life.

As a reminder, freedom here refers to man exercising his ability to create meaning for evading elusion. It is meaning confronting meaning, not the trading of one elusion for another. If a man previously eluded the absurd by being religious and then swaps religion with patriotism they are still being eluded. Freedom in this sense means one *consciously* crafts meaning to sharpen their understanding of the absurd.

Another reminder — just because the Absurdist commits the same action as an eluded man, that does not mean it is done for the same reasons. Our confrontation with the natural world is a meaning game, and the free man is capable of redefining all their actions to achieving lucidity. This is where our concept of freedom meets everyday life.

The free man can be impossible to distinguish based on their day-to-day actions. If you pass him in the street, there is nothing in his dress or demeanor that obviously gives him away. If you walk past his table at a restaurant his conversation will likely fail to turn heads. He needs no special vocation, and his demeanor at work may be practically normal. That is because freedom in this analysis is purely a mental exercise; it carries with it no mandate for anything in the material world. I do not have to dress a certain way or join a revolutionary organization. What I must do however is *think* and *reflect*.

This is where the everyday experience of the free man differs so much from the eluded. It requires direct consciousness on two fronts — first, by analyzing your own mind, and second, by analyzing the world about us. We will address each in turn.

Analyzing our own mind is important for maintaining lucidity of the absurd condition and avoiding the hijacking of our thoughts by the Natural Machine and/or Indoctrinated Self. This understanding of consciousness requires revisiting our determination of the soul. In Chapter 8, I define the soul as basically the interaction between the Natural Machine and the Indoctrinated Self (plus content). We do not challenge that formulation here. But what this conception leaves underdeveloped is the idea of consciousness. Near the start of this book I asserted that most individuals are rarely fully conscious; they simply drift through the cyclical process of the soul where their Natural Machine pulls their consciousness one way and the Indoctrinated Self supplements the experience. Such a life can be quite reflective, and individuals saturated in the world of confirmation and elusion are capable of producing reasonably complicated thought. But to be *truly* conscious the mind has to understand itself. It has to understand its processes, content, and the walls that enclose it. It is only when it understands its environment, characteristics, and above all its *potential* that it is capable of fully exercising its faculties.

Now this is not meant to imply that an individual will experience some nirvana or 'higher state of being' when they act this way. In fact, from my own personal experience, any feeling of elation or arousal is relatively short lived. It is also not a frame of mind that can be maintained. This part is especially important. Dependent on natural structures and existing in a natural world, consciousness is constantly shifting. Our experience of true consciousness is often brief and fleeting; it punctuates our thought rather than guiding it.

This assertion has consequences for how we understand our everyday existence. Contrary to Camus' demand that we remain constantly conscious[104], our mind is required by nature and society to focus on different things at different times. When I am at work, I am not free to keep my mind focused on the absurd; I must analyze numbers and laws and human behavior. Remember, our consciousness of the absurd is a *curse*, and we lack sufficient biological and mental structures to fully control our minds. Thus, I only experience my freedom sporadically throughout the workday. From time to time, when my Natural Machine demands a

---

[104] See *The Myth*, pages 53-54.

change in mental scenery, my thoughts transition to contemplating the absurd and exercising my freedom. The limited aspect of this capacity is unavoidable and to be expected. Those who truly understand the findings in this study will not be surprised by this restriction.

The consequence is we cannot maintain our lucid consciousness constantly during everyday life. The demands placed on our minds are too great; this is how Society force-feeds elusion down our throats. To survive I must go to work, pay bills, get gas for my car, and a million other things that overwhelm my thoughts before I can even consider reflecting on the character of the universe. This is when the re-interpretive qualities of freedom are most important.

Here is what the free man does. Establishing the maintenance of freedom as a priority in his life is the first step after awakening to it. It has to be something he cares about and something he is willing to devote mental energy toward. Next he must remember to actually exercise it. Memory — especially short term — is preoccupied throughout the day with satisfying this or that series of eluding tasks. It is usually being manipulated by the Natural Machine, not aiding any sort of 'higher thought'. The man seeking to exercise freedom must initially resort to reminders to do so. The memory must be forced, quite simply, to remember to be free. Once this is habitual however it becomes easier.

After these conditions are achieved the world becomes the free man's playground. Now nothing is safe from being reinterpreted either in his mind or outside it. Walking down the street, the behavior of his fellow men, the urban planning, this building's architecture all become victims of his thought. Purely natural phenomenon are no longer safe either; the breeze on his face and the rain on his coat are now further examples of how the natural world resists him.

This last sentence touches on the dangerousness of a free life. The free man runs the risk of reinterpreting everything in front of him as being *against him*. From the line at the grocery store to the red light at the intersection, everything he sees around him acts as a stop to his free behavior. A positive function of elusions for the 'normal' man is they impart a feeling of greater control over the world than he actually has. When the world is defined as following a system, then it can be predicted (except, of course, that it is unreasonable). The free man does not have this luxury. He knows the crime Nature committed against him; giving him awareness of his chains with no key to unlock them. It is in this state he is most oppressed and perhaps most vulnerable to self-annihilation.

Therefore, the free man can either: a) dive back into the sea of elusion, b) escape this cruel escapade through suicide, or c) learn to live with it. The first two are self-explanatory, and the third is given an unconvincing treatment by Camus[105]. So how does that third option work? My guess is differently for every man. What it requires from all however is creating meanings that make living in such a state sustainable. In one way this person is aided by the Natural Machine – it simply will not allow his thoughts to remain in this absurd climate forever. It provides a momentary respite. The word 'climate' is chosen deliberately to characterize this individual's experience. When one reaches and remains dedicated to freedom, this freedom becomes a "master frame"[106], or a primary reference the individual uses to interpret his life. It is important that this climate be not only flexible enough to account for the almost repeated interjections of the Natural Machine, but also hospitable enough for the person to survive it. While the occasional interruptions from the Natural Machine are not enough to maintain a person in this climate, they are capable of destroying this master frame if uncontrolled.

---

[105] See "The Myth of Sisyphus" chapter starting on page 119 in *The Myth*.
[106] Benford (2013).

This is where the redefinition of everyday events shows its importance. Yes, all of these events, objects, and people are against me; they constrain the free exercise of myself. But there is more to it than that. The capacity to transition beyond such a narrow state of mind is necessary for survival. First, the free man soon realizes that not everything is always against him. If this was the case, he would not realize his freedom in the first place. This or that book, mentor, or life experience led him to his current climate, not away from it. It worked with him to attain lucidity. Second, just because something is operating against you does not mean it is *bad*. There is no room for moral valuation in the absurd man's 'ethic'. All there is are situations that promote lucidity of his condition and those that do not. The quality of any given situation is irrelevant; all that matters is the individual's *willingness* to see it in a beneficial way.

Now the true character of freedom begins to take shape. I can do everything the common man does. I can go to work, eat dinner, watch a football game or a movie. But living in a free climate, I now *experience* it in a different way. Sure, I still become anxious before I do a presentation and excited when a team makes a touchdown, but my experience of life does not end there. Now, everything takes on vivid colors. I understand the meaning that a touchdown imparts, that taste of vicarious victory. I also understand how the anxiety of that presentation only strengthens my attachment to that occupation even more; it shows that some part of my mind cares about my job performance. In this climate, life is not just about experiencing, it is about experiencing *and* understanding. And often by understanding a situation, we experience it all the more profoundly.

Take romance movies. I love them. Here is the entire moral universe of what sexual relationships are *supposed to be*. Here there is so much meaning on parade, often including themes beyond structured reproduction, such as death, the 'meaning of life', the importance of relationships, and so on.

Living in the free climate I built for myself, I experience all the emotions associated with these meanings *even more*. I feel the lover's sacrifice so much more poignantly, because I *understand* it so much more poignantly. Specifically, I understand that the meaning he died for was fated to be temporary no matter what, and that makes his willing sacrifice all the more beautiful. Beauty to me is not a state or a structure, it is a *relationship*, and all the nuances of that relationship unfold before me all the more openly. I understand its function and importance, I understand its lifespan and temporary character, I understand how desperately it is wanted, and how profoundly it feels to acquire it regardless of how long it is held. I live, quite simply, more.

Another useful aspect of this climate is it allows me to see pitfalls. Society lays so many little traps for us along our journey. Elusion can appear so subtly and innocently to those who are not vigilant. The free man is tempted continuously to stray from the path. *Existentialism* is an excellent illustration of this, and perhaps the most dangerous. Here the same harrowing journey is undertaken, a man must pull himself out of the swamp of elusion, and cast his gaze across the landscape and into himself. But then there is always an escape clause; a cute little trick that reintroduces elusion into his life. Camus brilliantly illustrates multiple examples of this process in *The Myth*[107]. Here is the key difference between this existential analysis and the free man in this analysis. The free man does not care if another turns away. This is not a Sartrean attempt to propagate Communism. This form of living is part of a study, not a social movement. The free man running back to his captors is just an example of the contradictory behavior of nature and the lacking permanence

---

[107] For instance, when discussing Kierkegaard, Chestov, and other Existentialist philosophers.

of any state of life. There is no moral valuation attached to him, nor are there any loyalties.

Those instances where the consciousness looses freedom are also consequential for this analysis. For instance, there are those rare moments in everyday life where the natural world overwhelms the senses. These include situations such as painful injury, childbirth, excessive heat, etc. These instances of extreme pain or discomfort paralyze the Indoctrinated Self, and the Natural Machine rapidly rises to the forefront. The frequency of these experiences varies by an individual's society and the common situations they experience. In fact, they can be so common that they cease being rare. In a war zone for instance, death and dismemberment are so regular that the mind often treats them as standard phenomenon. This variability aside, we will examine a tamer example of this process in everyday life.

Take a heat wave. These are relatively uncommon on any given day. While time of year and geography certainly alter their frequency, the term is often relative and contingent on whatever temperature the individual is used to. Consider what happens to your cognition when exposed to this heat. Medical literature and personal experience tell me that my mind will begin to get 'fuzzy', I will become lethargic and my cognition will become cumbersome and harder to control. Before I know it, my mind is automatically directed toward certain topics, mainly how to get cool. In this situation the Natural Machine rises to the surface.

As discomfort and danger grow the power of the Natural Machine grows; at least in this situation. With body temperature rising, the fetters placed on it by the Indoctrinated Self loosen, and it takes increasingly exacting effort for my consciousness to control it. Additionally, as the Natural Machine rises in prominence, it is still decreasing in potency along with the rest of our mental and physical abilities. This is why individuals with heat stroke often behave as if drunk; the natural aspect is mostly controlling cognition, yet it is too weak to act with normal efficacy.

Some of you may call this 'instinct', but it is far more complex than a simple reaction. We do not just run away or attack something. Society does not allow situations to be as simple as that; meaning is everywhere, and even though my Indoctrinated Self may be barely operating in severe instances, our society still arranges settings and situations to constrain behavior. I cannot punch my way out of a hot room when I am heat exhausted. Nor can I raid a locked shipping container when I am on the brink of starvation. In these instances, while the Natural Machine hijacks consciousness and orients thought toward immediate resolutions of the situation, that situation will still always constrain the available actions socially and materially.

So what about when the Natural Machine *cannot* resolve these situations? What does it do when we are stuck in that hot cinderblock room, and we know we cannot get out for another hour? In these instances the Natural Machine appears to plunge our consciousness *inside*. In such an unbearable physical situation, it seeks to find some bearable mental situation. It rifles through our memories and desires, and starts orienting our mind toward them. In essence, it seeks to elude us from our helpless situation. For example, I once was stuck at work when the heating system malfunctioned during the dead of winter. With the boiler running nonstop, it reached over ninety degrees in some rooms. Unable to leave, I was forced to sit at my station and rub my arms and neck with water to cool myself. After a few hours, I became delirious. Knowing that it could not get me out of the situation, my Natural Machine looked for potent elusions to distract me from the reality of the present. I stopped analyzing the situation as a manifestation of the absurd, with nature acting on me regardless of my desires, and instead I found myself thinking about fishing that weekend. It was *all* I could think about actually, to the point where I was simply thinking about walleye swimming in front of me. Life became like a dream, and I still cannot recall everything that happened that day while in my deluded state.

So far, this section discussed the notion of freedom at great length. But there are other consequences for daily life in this analysis. The last I will discuss is the *experience of time*. How do the results of this investigation and Absurdism in general impact our experience of time in and beyond our 'normal' day?

For the 'regular' man, time either transpires quickly or slowly. After doing something enjoyable, people often say time "flew by". When it is something onerous, time "drags". It is a tragedy really. When you consider such a state, the eluded man does not enjoy the positive aspects of his life as much as the negative. Even though the time spent in each may be *exactly* the same, the way this man *experiences* these situations is highly unbalanced. Either they transpire too quickly for him to enjoy them or they become boring. Adding to the tragedy of the situation, if a man engages in a desired behavior too much it becomes *undesirable*. As discussed earlier, the Natural Machine demands change, and the things we enjoy the most at any moment are often those that are *novel*. But once the novelty wears off, and once the enjoyed object or process creeps closer to being a *constant*, the love is lost.

The everyday therefore for the eluded man is a tragedy. But this is not the only way he experiences time. There is also the matter of his past and future, or what Camus relegates to *nostalgia* and *hope*, respectively. As previously discussed, the Natural Machine often recalls memories throughout the day. These in turn contribute to elusion by infusing meaning from the past into daily life. Memories of childhood and times of good or bad augment his experience of time in the present. They assign valuations to current endeavors, and often shape what endeavors the individual chooses to initiate. These valuations have an influence on how the individual experiences time, often aiding the establishment of 'flow'[108] during the event.

Hopes for the future also augment an individual's experience of time. As examined by Camus, these hopes shape the behaviors individuals choose to engage in and how they evaluate various scenarios. This also has a significant impact on the experience of time beyond simple daydreaming. The overall path of life that hope places a man on will have significant consequences for his *daily* life. His vocation, living situation, pursuits and passions, etc. all impact how quickly or slowly his days transpire. A man often oriented toward the future will *rush* to it and thereby, as Camus asserts, also rush to his death.

Thus, for the eluded man, nature simply does not allow him to have too much fun. Luckily, modern society provides him with a host of playthings to satisfy his demand for novelty, but these are all fated to eventually wilt. The free, absurd man looks on with pity. In the present we find everything we need. Regardless of the familiarity or barrenness of our surroundings there is variation everywhere. One simply needs to know how to look. Living with our curse frees us from the interference of the past and the future. Sure, the present can take on the characteristic of hell for us, confronting us with our absurd condition. But to the man oriented toward truth, the hell of the present is favorable to a future built on desires rarely fulfilled. I prefer what I know, not what I hope, and I know this moment will pass like all the others in a universe without definite meaning or value.

In the end, does it matter that we have such vision, that we are free? Does it matter that we can see the tyranny of the natural so clearly, and feel it so profoundly? *No*, because as far as I can tell, nothing matters. Living a life 'without appeal' means living only with what you know. I know very little. But it never ceases to amaze me. What little I know is so

---

[108] See Csíkszentmihályi (1975).

manifold in its complexity. Coupled with the almost infinite universe of meaning man creates in response to our human condition, there is enough to experience and examine for multiple lifetimes. Sure, the absurd is a curse, but just because someone is cursed does not mean their life is all writhing and torment. Even Frankenstein got to play with flowers.

This chapter reviewed but a few consequences of this analysis in relatively superficial fashion. There are many more equally demanding of attention. The important conclusion to take away from this chapter is the broad applicability of this analysis. It is not only a natural or social analysis, nor is it purely discursive or immaterial. It is also not entirely consistent. Such interpretive power does however necessitate further study, and has the potential to increase what little understanding we have.

IX) Conclusion

Now we come to the close of this analysis. What did we learn?

First, the absurdist methodology is a powerful analytical tool. Inductive study that relies solely on experiential knowledge is capable of increasing our understanding of natural and social processes. In this analysis, we applied this method to understand the structure and function of our minds, and in turn increased our understanding of the structure and function of nature and society. By intensively scrutinizing ourselves and the world about us, an analysis focusing on one area of human experience is capable of shedding light on other processes. The absurdist methodology therefore rejects the current sectarian nature of social science, focusing its gaze on macro social processes that shape existence while shunning attempts at myopic, trivial theorization of specific social processes and objects. We care about experience as a whole, and even when examining a single aspect of experience (the mind), this methodology reveals findings of general applicability beyond current theoretical frameworks.

Building on this theme, our second lesson is this: everything is connected. This statement is not meant to infuse this investigation with an element of mysticism. This is not a pedantic attempt at articulating a humanism or some universal morality. What it means is for the scientist to thoroughly understand one aspect of the world they must understand others. When it comes to society and the social aspects of man, determining their connection to the natural world is of significant importance.

The natural drives all the processes discussed in this text. It fuels the Natural Machine of each individual which, desiring confirmation and domination over nature, gives rise to an entire universe of social objects. This includes groups, organizations, institutions, and societies. Continuing their mission to hold constant what can never be held constant, these social objects are socialized into the individual, giving rise to the Indoctrinated Self. This in turn seeks to constrain the individual Natural Machine, attempting to force consistency down its throat. While all these social efforts inevitably fail, it is important to remember they are natural creations themselves. Emblematic of the contradictory character of the natural, it created the very objects and individuals that seek to imprison it.

Everything is connected, and everything is confused. I attempted to trace a faint outline of this dynamic between the social and the natural, but any intent to create a true likeness is a fool's endeavor. The concepts and analysis I produced in these pages is incorrect, contradictory, limited, and soon surpassed. The natural world will not allow its secrets to be understood. All we have are approximations, which is fine if these are not confused with truth. Unfortunately, what makes the absurdist method so novel is its refusal to partake in this very confusion that modern science is all too eager to adopt.

Third, this analysis entails significant consequences for multiple concepts that are loaded with social importance. The question of the soul is engaged, along with other themes such as time and eternal life. Sometimes, the findings it produces may seem contrary to what was expected at the onset; a fine illustration of nature's unreasonable character. The result is a study that openly embraces the capacity to *surprise* the investigator. There is no place for structured hypotheses and models here. What is required is the *bravery* to study morally-loaded topics, and the *tenacity* to stick with the method. My method approaches the world with as few expectations as possible. It is a desire to maintain this methodology, not to find a desirable outcome, that characterizes the spirit of this book.

I could go on and on, cataloguing the scores of impacts and contributions this text supposedly makes to our understanding. But all these will be ignored or forgotten anyway; nature does not allow us to hold onto things for long. To close this book, I think it is more interesting to reflect on its title. Now it is clear. A specific image of man comes to light. He is not some product of providence nor is he simply an evolved bacterium. He is the embodied *Variance* of nature, a confluence of chaos from the natural world and meaning from the social world. He is also afraid of this variance, and through his immense desire to fix himself, to hold himself *constant*, he creates grand elusions. This is perhaps the most significant attribute that separates humans from the rest of nature. Faced with the natural, we construct a brilliant society for our minds and our world.

I sought to show how perplexing and complex we are and our creations are. I leave it to the reader to determine if I was successful.

X) Works Cited

Barkan, Steven E. 2013. *Social problems: continuity and change.* Washington D.C.: Flat World Knowledge.

Becker, Howard. 1997. *Outsiders: Studies In The Sociology Of Deviance.* New York: Free Press.

Bekoff, Marc. 2002. "Animal reflections". *Nature,* 419: 255.

Benford, Robert D. 2013. "Master Frame" in *The Wiley Blackwell Encyclopedia of Social & Political Movements.* Hoboken: Wiley.

Bernstein, DM and EF Loftus. 2009. "How to tell if a particular memory is true or false". *Perspectives in Psychological Science,* 4(4): 370-4.

Bourdieu, Pierre. 1984. *Distinction: a social critique of the judgement of taste.* London: Routledge.

Camus, Albert. 1995. *A Happy Death.* Trans. R. Howard. New York: Vintage.

———. 1992. *The Rebel: An Essay on Man in Revolt.* Trans. A. Bower. New York: Vintage.

———. 1991. *The Myth of Sisyphus and Other Essays.* Trans. J. O'Brien. New York: Vintage.

Cholbi, Michael. 2017. "Suicide". *Stanford Encyclopedia of Philosophy.* Stanford: Stanford Center for the Study of Language and Information.

Csíkszentmihályi, Mihály. 1975. *Beyond boredom and anxiety.* Hoboken: Jossey-Bass Publishers.

Dostoevsky, Fyodor. 1995. *Demons: A Novel in Three Parts.* Trans R. Pevear and L. Volokhonsky. New York: Vintage Classics.

Fausto-Sterling, 2000. *Sexing the Body: Gender Politics and the Construction of Sexuality.* New York: Basic Books.

Federal Bureau of Investigation. 2017. *2016: Crime in the United States.* Washington D.C.: U.S. Department of Justice. <https://ucr.fbi.gov/crime-in-the-u.s/2016/crime-in-the-u.s.-2016>.

Feynman, Richard P., Robert B. Leighton, and Matthew Sands. 1977. *The Feynman Lectures on Physics, Vol. 1: Mainly Mechanics, Radiation, and Heat.* 1st ed. Boston: Addison-Wesley.

Foucault, Michel. 1995. *Discipline & Punish: The Birth of the Prison.* Trans. A. Sheridan. New York: Vintage.

Goethe, Johann Wolfgang von. 2008. *Faust, Part One.* Trans. D. Luke. Oxford: Oxford UP.

Goffman, Erving. 1974. *Frame Analysis.* Cambridge: Harvard UP.

Gurney, Joan Neff and Kathleen J. Tierney. 1982. "Relative Deprivation and Social Movements: A Critical Look at Twenty Years of Theory and Research". *The Sociological Quarterly*, 23(1): 33-47.

Hartmann, Heidi I. 1979. "The Unhappy Marriage of Marxism and Feminism: Towards a more Progressive Union". *Capital & Class*, 3(2): 1-33.

Kaufmann, Walter. 1974. *Nietzsche: Philosopher, Psychologist, Antichrist.* 4th ed. Princeton: Princeton UP.

Kautsky, Karl. 1919. *Terrorism and Communism: A Contribution to the Natural History of Revolution.* Manchester: National Labour Press.

Knoke, David, George W. Bohrnstedt, and Alisa Potter Mee. 2002. *Statistics for Social Data Analysis.* 4th ed. Belmont: Wadsworth/Thomson Learning.

Latour, Bruno. 1988. *Science in Action: How to Follow Scientists and Engineers through Society.* Cambridge: Harvard UP.

Mead, George Herbert. 1934. *Mind, Self, and Society: From the Standpoint of a Social Behaviorist.* Ed. C.W. Morris. Chicago: University of Chicago Press.

McAdam, Doug. 1999. *Political Process and the Development of Black Insurgency, 1930-1970.* Chicago: University of Chicago Press.

Merton, Robert K. 1938. "Social Structure and Anomie". *American Sociological Review*, 3(5): 672-682.

Nathan, John. 2000. *Mishima: A Biography*. Cambridge, MA: Da Capo Press.

Nietzsche, Friedrich. 1989. *Beyond Good and Evil: Prelude to a Philosophy of the Future*. Trans. W. Kaufmann. New York: Vintage.

Parker, Ashley and Robert Costa. 2017. "'Everyone tunes in': Inside Trump's obsession with cable TV". *The Washington Post*: 4/23/2017. < https://www.washingtonpost.com/politics/everyone-tunes-in-inside-trumps-obsession-with-cable-tv/2017/04/23/3c52bd6c-25e3-11e7-a1b3-faff0034e2de_story.html?utm_term=.767a765078e2>.

Pasha-Robinson, Lucy. 2017. "Nato officials will 'ensure no one talks for more than four minutes to keep Donald Trump's attention'". *The Independent*: 5/16/2017. <http://www.independent.co.uk/news/world/americas/nato-donald-trump-four-minute-time-limit-keep-us-president-attention-span-meeting-a7738626.html>.

Proudhon, Pierre-Joseph. 2008. *What is Property?: An Inquiry into the Principle of Right and of Government*. London: Forgotten Books.

Rosenwald, Michael S. 2018. "Trump isn't big on reading. Teddy Roosevelt consumed whole books before breakfast". *The Washington Post*. < https://www.washingtonpost.com/news/retropolis/wp/2018/01/09/trump-isnt-big-on-reading-teddy-roosevelt-consumed-whole-books-before-breakfast/?utm_term=.d1398995ae35>.

Saldana, Justin. 2013. "Power and Conformity in Today's Schools". *International Journal of Humanities and Social Science*, 3(1): 228-32.

Simmel, Georg. 1969. "The Metropolis and Mental Life" in *Classic Essays on the Culture of Cities*. Ed. R. Sennett. Englewood Cliffs: Prentice-Hall.

Subramuniyaswami, Sivaya. 1992. "Let's Talk About Suicide". *Hinduism Today*. <https://www.hinduismtoday.com/modules/smartsection/item.php?itemid=985>.

Stryker, Sheldon and Peter J. Burke. 2000. "The Past, Present, and Future of an Identity Theory". *Social Psychology Quarterly*, 63(4): 284-297.

Weber, Max. 1958. *From Max Weber: Essays in Sociology*. Eds. H.H. Gerth and C.W. Mills. Oxford: Oxford UP.

Wells, Gary L. and Elizabeth A. Olson. 2003. "Eyewitness Testimony". *Annual Review of Psychology*, 54: 277-95.

Printed in Great Britain
by Amazon

84797935R00080